MILITARY HIS [

PRIMARY S

WATERLOO 1815

CAPTAIN MERCER'S JOURNAL

EDITED BY

W.H. FITCHETT, B.A., L.L.D.

With an introduction by Bob Carruthers

Pen & Sword
MILITARY

This edition published in 2012 by
Pen & Sword Military
An imprint of
Pen & Sword Books Ltd
47 Church Street
Barnsley
South Yorkshire
S70 2AS

First published in Great Britain in 2011 in digital format by
Coda Books Ltd.

ISBN 978 1 78159 146 8

This book contains an extract from: 'Wellington's Men', edited by W.H. Fitchett, B.A., L.L.D.
Published by George Bell and Sons Limited, 1900

A CIP catalogue record for this book is
available from the British Library

Printed and bound by CPI Group (UK) Ltd, Croydon, CR0 4YY

Pen & Sword Books Ltd incorporates the Imprints of Pen & Sword Aviation, Pen & Sword Family History, Pen & Sword Maritime, Pen & Sword Military, Pen & Sword Discovery, Pen & Sword Politics, Pen & Sword Atlas, Pen & Sword Archaeology, Wharncliffe Local History, Wharncliffe True Crime, Wharncliffe Transport, Pen & Sword Select, Pen & Sword Military Classics, Leo Cooper, The Praetorian Press, Claymore Press, Remember When, Seaforth Publishing and Frontline Publishing

For a complete list of Pen & Sword titles please contact
PEN & SWORD BOOKS LIMITED
47 Church Street, Barnsley, South Yorkshire, S70 2AS, England
E-mail: enquiries@pen-and-sword.co.uk
Website: www.pen-and-sword.co.uk

CONTENTS

INTRODUCTION

The journals of Captain Cavalie Mercer provide us with a unique insight into the events of this most famous of military campaigns from a rare point of view.

There are many accounts of life in Wellington's armies as told from the perspective of those serving in the ranks of the infantry and the cavalry. This highly interesting account comes from the point of an artilleryman commanding a battery of guns. Mercer was in the very thick of the action and is able to provide us with an exciting and detailed account of some of the most important incidents in the battle. It is interesting to speculate what might have happened had Mercer and his battery not been present to oppose the French cavalry charges and add their firepower to the infantry engagements.

I first came across the account of Cavalie Mercer when I was producing the "Campaigns In History" series for Discovery channel. The series featured the insights of the late great Doctor David Chandler, author of "The Campaign's Of Napoleon" which is still regarded as the definitive work on the Emperor Napoleon in English, and it was he who first introduced me to the delights of Captain Mercer's Journal. I trust that the reader in search of an engaging primary source perspective will gain as much satisfaction as I did from discovering these wonderful recollections.

Mercer had a talent as an artist which appears to have a arisen from his splendid eye for detail. He was clearly an outstanding observer and the result is an intriguing and absorbing journal which is rich in both incident and detail. The original plan for this series was for me to annotate sections of Mercer's Journal in order to produce a primary source account of the campaign with a commentary from a modern perspective. However once I got down to the pleasure of revisiting the Mercer Journal, I also recalled the work of Fitchett entitled "Wellington's Men". In producing new annotations I soon realised I would have been largely going over exactly the same ground which Fitchett had covered over a century before me. Looking at "Wellington's Men" afresh for the first time in 20 years I was struck by the quaintness of the Victorian turn of phrase and the unashamed celebration of the actions of men of Waterloo. I soon came to the conclusion that Fitchett, being much nearer in time to the events he described, had its own validity as a historical document.

Mercer's diaries require some degree of explanation and Fitchett in the pages of "Wellington's Men" did an exceptional job of presenting the key elements of those diaries to his own Victorian audience. I have therefore opted to provide the reader with an edited version Fitchett's work in the hope that the reader will gain a fresh insight into the battle of Waterloo not just through the eyes of a participant who played a pivotal role in the events, but also how those events were presented to a Victorian audience at a time when the British Empire was it its height.

Thank you for buying this book and I sincerely hope that you enjoy discovering the work of both Mercer and Fitchett.

Bob Carruthers 2011

ALEXANDER CAVALIÉ MERCER
(28TH MARCH 1783 – 9TH NOVEMBER 1868)

THE SOLDIER IN LITERATURE

This volume is an attempt to rescue from undeserved oblivion a soldierly autobiography; and to give to the general reader a picture of a famous battle, not as described by the historian or analysed by the philosopher, but as seen by the eyes of men who fought in them. History treats the men who do the actual fighting in war very ill. It commonly forgets all about them. If it occasionally sheds a few drops of careless ink upon them, it is without either comprehension or sympathy. From the orthodox historian's point of view, the private soldier is a mere unconsidered pawn in the passionless chess of some cold-brained strategist. As a matter of fact a battle is an event which pulsates with the fiercest human passions - passions bred of terror and of daring; of the anguish of wounds and of the rapture of victory; of the fear and awe of human souls over whom there suddenly sweeps the mystery of death.

But under conventional literary treatment all this evaporates. To the historian a battle is as completely drained of human emotion as a chemical formula. It is evaporated into a haze of cold and cloudy generalities.

But this is certainly to miss what is, for the human imagination, the most characteristic feature of a great fight. A battle offers the spectacle of, say, a hundred thousand men lifted up suddenly and simultaneously into a mood of intensest passion - heroic or diabolical - eager to kill and willing to be killed; a mood in which death and wounds count for nothing and victory for everything. This is the feature of war which stirs the common imagination of the race; which makes gentle women weep, and wise philosophers stare, and the average hot-blooded human male turn half-frenzied with excitement. What does each separate human atom feel, when caught in that whirling tornado of passion and of peril? Who shall make visible to us the actual faces in the fighting- line; or make audible the words stern order, broken prayer, blasphemous jest spoken amid the tumult? Who shall give us, in a word, an adequate picture of the soldier's life in actual war-time, with its hard- ships, its excitements, its escapes, its exultation and despair?

If the soldier attempts to tell the tale himself he commonly fails. In ninety-nine cases out of a hundred he belongs to the inarticulate classes. He lacks the gift of description. He can do a great deed, but cannot describe it when it is done. If knowledge were linked in them to an adequate gift of literary expression, soldiers would be the great literary artists of the race. For who else lives through so wide and so wild a range of experience and emotion. When, as in the case of Napier, a soldier emerges with a distinct touch of literary genius, the result is an immortal book. But usually the soldier has to be content with making history; he leaves to others the tamer business of writing it, and generally himself suffers the injustice of being forgotten in the process. Literature is congested with books which describe the soldier from the outside; which tell the tale of his hardships and heroisms, his follies and vices, as they are seen by the remote and uncomprehending spectator. What the world needs is the tale of the bayonet and of 'Brown Bess,' written by the hand which has actually used those weapons.

Now, the narrative which these pages offer afresh to the world is of exactly this character. It is pages of battle-literature written by the hands of a soldier. It is not an attempt at history, but an exercise in auto-biography. So it is an actual human document, with the salt of truth, of sincerity, and of reality in every syllable. The faded leaves of this memoir is still stained with the red wine of battle. In these words - to the imaginative and sympathetic hearer, at all events - these are still audible the shouts of charging men, the roll of musketry volleys, the earth-shaking thunder of Waterloo. Passages from Mercer's experiences in command of a battery at Waterloo are woven into the pages of this book. This book old and form a rare prize to be picked up by the fortunate collector in second-hand bookshops. Mercer's 'Journal of the Waterloo Campaign' was written in 1830, and published as late as 1870. But it consists of two volumes, in which the story of the great battle is only an episode, and it has never reached any wide circle of readers. Yet Mercer's account of Waterloo is the best personal narrative of the great fight in English literature.

This book is thus of rare interest and value. It belongs to the era of 'Brown Bess,' and of Waterloo. Mercer commanded battery G - fondly described by its Captain as "the finest troop in the service" - at Waterloo. Mercer was a fighting man of the highest quality. Mercer fought his battery at Waterloo until, out of 200 fine horses in his troop, 140 lay dead or dying; while of the men not enough survived to man four guns; and these, as the great battle came to its end, fell, smoke-blackened and exhausted, in slumber beside their blood- splashed guns. He had, in an amusing degree, an intense pride in the particular body to which he belonged. The army with him counted for little, the regiment was everything.

Captain Mercer, an educated man, plainly cherishes a hearty belief that battery G has the finest horses, the best equipment, the smartest men, and the most perfect discipline, not merely in the British army, but in any army known to history! Pride in the regiment to which the soldier happens to belong is a fine element of military strength. Under modern short-service conditions it grows faint; but amongst Wellington's veterans it had almost the fervours of a religion.

It may be added that this writer is curiously distinct, and looks at war through very diverse eyes. Mercer represents a type of officer in which the British army of all days is rich; and whose qualities explain some of the failures, and most of the triumphs of that army. He was gallant in every drop of his blood; cool, hardy, athletic, a fit leader of the fighting line. He had been reared in luxury, accustomed to feed daintily every day, to lie softly every night; he was full of the pride of his caste; yet in the actual business of fighting, Mercer, like all officers of the type to which he belonged, could outmarch the privates in the ranks. He fared as hardly as they, shared their scanty rations, lay like them on the wet soil, endured in every way as much, and grumbled less. He was not only first in the charge, but last in the retreat, and took it all - hunger, wet, cold, perils - with smiling face, as part of the day's work.

The British private was by no means an angel in a red coat. His vices, like his virtues, were of a primitive sort. He drank, he swore, and alas, he plundered. If the valour which raged at the great breach of Badajos, or swept up the slope of rugged stones at San Sebastian, was of almost incredible fire, so the brutality which plundered and ravished and slew after the city was carried, was of almost incredible fierceness.

Mercer is an able and most accomplished writer. He belonged to the scientific branch of the army, the artillery, and he had studied his art with the thoroughness of a scholar. That Mercer was a cool and gallant soldier of the finest type cannot be doubted. He has, indeed, a fine military record, and rose to the rank of general, and held command of the 9th Brigade of Royal Artillery. But Mercer was a many-sided man in a quite curious degree. He was a scholar; a lover of books; a country gentleman, with a country gentleman's delight in horse-flesh and crops. He was, moreover, an artist, with a Ruskinesque, not to say a Turneresque, sense of colour and form. A fine landscape was for him a feast, only rivalled by the joy of a good book. He lingers on the very edge of Quatre Bras, while the thunder of cannon shakes the air, and while his own guns are floundering up a steep hill path, to note and describe the far-stretching landscape, the glow of the evening sky, the Salvator-like trees, the sparkle of glassy pools, &c. Mercer is so good an artillery officer that he sees every buckle in the harness of his horses, and every button on the uniforms of his men; and yet he is sensitive to every tint and change in the landscape through which his guns are galloping.

On the morning after Waterloo, his face still black with its smoke, and his ears stunned with its roar, he picks his way across the turf, thick with the bodies of the slain, into the garden of Hougoumont. The bodies of the dead lie there, too; but Mercer is almost intoxicated with the cool verdure of the trees, with the chant of a stray nightingale, and even with "the exuberant vegetation of turnips and cabbages," as well as with the scent of flowers! It is this combination of keen artistic sensibility with the finest type of courage courage which, if gentle in form, was yet of the ice-brook's temper which makes Mercer interesting. Here was a man who might have fished with Izaak Walton, or discussed hymns with Cowper, or philosophy with Coleridge; yet this pensive, gentle, artistic, bookish man fought G Battery at Waterloo till two-thirds of his troop were killed, and has written the best account of the great battle, from the human and personal side, to be found in English literature.

Here, then, is a human document, of genuine historic value, as well as of keen personal interest. It has its defects. There is no perspective in its pages. This memoir will not give the reader the battle as a whole; still less the campaign; least of all will it give the politics behind the campaign. But a magic is in it, the magic of reality and of personal experience. It seems to put the reader in the actual battle-line, to fill his nostrils with the scent of gunpowder, to make his eyes tingle with the pungency of ancient battle-smoke.

It may be added that this book gives pictures of such battle landscapes as will never be witnessed again. It belongs to the period when war had much more of the picturesque and human element than it has to-day. 'Brown Bess' was short of range, and the fighting-lines came so near to each other that each man could see his foeman's face, and hear his shout or oath. War appealed to every sense. It filled the eyes. It registered itself in drifting continents of smoke. It deafened the ear with blast of cannon and ring of steel. It adorned itself in all the colours of the rainbow. The uniforms of Napoleon's troops, as they were drawn up on the slopes of La Belle Alliance, were a sort of debauch of colour. Houssaye gives a catalogue of the Regiments - infantry of the line in blue coats, white breeches, and gaiters; heavy cavalry with glittering cuirasses and pennoned lances; chasseurs in green and purple and yellow; hussars with dolmans and shakos of all tints - sky-blue, scarlet, green, and red; dragoons with white shoulder-belts and turban-helmets of tiger-skin, surmounted by a gleaming cone of brass; lancers in green, with silken cords on their helmets; carabineers, giants of six feet, clad in white, with breastplates of gold and lofty helmets with red plumes; grenadiers in blue, faced with scarlet, yellow epaulettes, and high bear-skin caps; the red lancers - red-breeched, red-capped, with floating white plumes half a yard long; the Young Guard; the Old Guard, with bearskin helmets, blue trousers and coats ; the artillery of the Guard, with bear-skin helmets, &c.

Such a host, looked at from the picturesque point of view, was a sort of human rainbow, with a many-coloured gleam of metal - gold and silver, steel and Brass - added. And colour counts at least in attracting recruits. Lord Roberts has told the world how he joined the Bengal Horse Artillery purely because he found their white buckskin breeches, and the leopard skin and red plumes on the men's helmets, irresistible! Napoleon, it will be remembered, turned the spectacular aspect of his army to martial use. On the morning of Waterloo he brought his troops over the slope of the hill in eleven stately columns; he spread them out like a mighty glittering fan in the sight of the coolly watching British. To foes of more sensitive imagination the spectacle of that vast and iris-tinted host might well have chilled their courage. But the

British whether to their credit or their discredit may be disputed keep their imagination and their courage in separate compartments. They are not liable to be discouraged, still less put to rout, by the most magnificent display of what may be called the millinery of war.

But that aspect of war has faded, never to revive. Khaki kills the picturesque. Battle has grown grey, remote, invisible. It consists of trenches miles long, in which crouch unseen riflemen, shooting at moving specks of grey, distant thousands of yards; or in guns perched on hills five miles apart bellowing to each other across the intervening valleys. It is not merely that in a battle of today a soldier cannot see the features of the man he kills; he probably does not see him at all. The Highlanders at the Modder marched, panted, thirsted, killed, and were killed, for eight hours, and never saw a Boer! The soldier today sees neither the pin-pricks of flame nor the whiff of grey smoke which tell that somebody is shooting at him. For these are days of smokeless powder and long-range rifles. The man shot at only learns that circumstance as he catches the air-scurry of the passing bullet, and the atmosphere about him grows full of what one half-terrified war correspondent calls "little whimpering air-devils."

The interest of these books is that they bring back to us living pictures, as seen through living human eyes, of the great battles of a century ago - battles which have grown obsolete in fashion, but which changed the currents of the world's history, and of whose gain we are the heirs today.

It is curious, in a sense even amusing, to note how his famous commander impressed this soldier, occupied in recording for the benefit of posterity what he saw.

Mercer came close to the great Duke, and regards him with a cooler and therefore a severer judgment. Mercer had boundless confidence in Wellington as a battle-leader, but not the least affection for him as a man, and it is plain he had no special reasons for affection. Wellington had many fine moral qualities, but anxious consideration for other people, or even calm justice in his dealings with them, is not to be included in their catalogue. The famous general order he issued after the retreat from Burgos is an example of the undiscriminating harshness with which Wellington could treat an entire army. And that element of harshness - of swift, impatient, relentless discipline that could not stay to discriminate, to weigh evidence, or even to hear it - was one great defect of Wellington as a general. About his soldiers he had as little human feeling as a good chess-player has about his pawns. Mercer never came into intercourse with the Duke but with disaster to himself, a disaster edged with injustice.

When his troop was in France, Mercer says he ran an equal risk of falling under the Duke's displeasure for systematically plundering the farmers, or for not plundering them! If a commander of a battery allowed his horses to look in worse condition than those of another battery he was relentlessly punished. "The quick eye of the Duke would see the difference. He asked no questions, attended to no justification, but condemned the unfortunate captain as unworthy of the command he held, and perhaps sent him from the army." But the official amount of forage supplied was quite insufficient for the purpose of keeping the horses in high condition. Other troops supplemented the supply by 'borrowing' from the farmers, and there was no resource but to imitate them, or to risk professional ruin by presenting at parade horses inferior in look to those of other troops nourished on mere felony. Wellington forgave neither the unlicensed "borrowing" of the officers nor the want of condition in their horses. Yet one fault or the other was inevitable.

The Duke, it seems, "had no love for the artillery," and all his harshness was expended on that branch of the service." The Duke of Wellington's ideas of discipline," says Mercer, "are rigid; his modes of administering them are summary, and he is frequently led into acts of the grossest injustice." Thus the owner of a building where some of Mercer's men were quartered - a thorough rogue - complained to the Duke that the lead piping of his house had been plundered and sold by the guilty British gunners. Wellington made no inquiry, took no evidence. A staff officer rode to Mercer's quarters one day with a copy of this complaint, on the margin of which was written in the

Duke's own handwriting: "Colonel Scovell will find out whose troop this is, and they shall pay double." This was the first intimation the unfortunate Mercer had received of the charge against him. The Frenchman pretended to estimate his loss at 7000 francs, and Mercer was advised, in high quarters, to pay this sum in order to escape the Duke's wrath. Mercer appealed to Sir George Wood, who told him his only chance lay in evading payment as long as he could; then the Duke might be caught in a more amiable mood. The actual thief - one of the French villagers - was discovered and convicted; but this circumstance, Mercer records, "has not in the least altered my position with the Duke of Wellington; for none dare tell him the story; and even Sir Edward Barnes, who kindly attempted it, met with a most ungracious rebuff!"

The French scoundrel, meanwhile, was dunning Mercer to get his 7000 francs. The situation remained thus for weeks, till the audacious Frenchman ventured on a second interview with the Duke. The Duke had dismounted, as it happened, in a very ill humour, at the door of his hotel, and the Frenchman pursued him up the grand staircase with his complaint. The Duke turned roughly upon him, "What the devil do you want, sir?" The Frenchman presented his bill with a flourish, whereupon the Duke exclaimed to his aide-de-camp, "Pooh! kick the rascal downstairs!" The Frenchman and his bill thus vanished from the scene; but Mercer's comment is "that I eventually escaped paying a heavy sum for depredations committed by others is due, not to the Duke's sense of justice, but only to the irritability of his temper."

On another occasion Sir Augustus Fraser, meeting him, said, "Mercer, you are released from arrest." Mercer stared: but on inquiry, discovered that he had been officially under arrest for a fortnight without knowing it. At a review, just before passing the saluting point, a horse in the rear division of his battery got its leg over the trace. The limber gunners leaped smartly off, put things straight, and jumped to their places again; but the division, with their 18-pounders, had to trot to regain place, and were just pulling up when they reached the saluting point. The precise and rhythmical order of the troop was a little disturbed, and Wellington, in a burst of wrath, put Sir Augustus Fraser himself, who was in command of all the artillery, the major in command of the brigade, and Mercer, the captain of the guilty troop, under arrest, where - happily all unconscious - they remained for a fortnight. Later Mercer wished to apply for leave of absence, but Sir George Wood declined to present the request, as he said, "'It would not be prudent just now to remind the Duke of me in any way.' Rather hard and unjust this," is Mercer's comment.

Mercer, however, tells one story, which shows that the Duke of Wellington was capable of sly satire at the expense of the French. An English officer walking on the boulevard was rudely pushed into the gutter by a French gentleman, whom the Englishman promptly knocked down. The Frenchman, it turned out, was a marshal. He complained to the Duke, but could not identify the officer who had knocked him down. The Duke there-upon issued a general order, desiring that "British officers would, in future, abstain from beating marshals of France."

W.H. Fitchett, B.A., L.L.D.

ARTHUR WELLESLEY, 1ST DUKE OF WELLINGTON
Francisco de Goya 1812 - 1814

CHAPTER I

WAITING FOR THE GUNS

Mercer held the rank of second captain only in troop G, but Sir Alexander Dickson, whose troop it was, being employed on other duties, Mercer was in actual command. It was a fine troop, perfect in drill, and splendidly horsed. It owed this latter circumstance, perhaps, to a characteristic bit of War Office administration. The artillery was being reduced to the level of a peace establishment when Napoleon broke loose from Elba, and there came the sudden summons to war. A second troop of horse-artillery was at that moment in Colchester barracks. It was broken up, and troop G took the picked horses of both batteries "thus," says Mercer proudly, "making it the finest troop in the service." One fine troop was in this way made out of two half-dismantled batteries.

The troop was made up of eighty gunners and eighty-four drivers, with the usual proportion of officers and non-commissioned officers. The horses numbered no less than 226. There were six guns five of them being nine-pounders, and one a heavy five-and-a-half inch howitzer. Mercer has the wholesome pride of a good officer in his own men and guns. He tells with pardonable complacency the story of how his troop shone in a grand cavalry review held on May 29, near Gramont:-

"About two o'clock the Duke of Wellington and Prince Blucher, followed by an immense cortege, in which were to be seen many of the most distinguished officers and almost every uniform in Europe, arrived on the ground. Need I say that the foreigners were loud in praise of the martial air,

"THE WHOLE LINE WILL ADVANCE!"
Lord Wellington, at seven o'clock, after the repulse of the Old Guard, stood up in his stirrups, and, taking his hat off, cried, "The whole line will advance!"
Drawn by B. Catus Woodville. Published by The Illustrated London News.

fine persons, and complete equipment of the men and horses, and of the strength and beauty of the latter? and my vanity on that occasion was most fully gratified, for on arriving where we stood, the Duke not only called old Blucher's attention to 'the beautiful battery,' but, instead of proceeding straight through the ranks, as they had done everywhere else, each subdivision nay, each individual horse was closely scrutinised, Blucher repeating continually that he had never seen anything so superb in his life, and concluding by exclaiming, 'Mein Gott, dere is not von orse in dies batterie wich is not goot for Veldt Marshal': and Wellington agreed with him. It certainly was a splendid collection of horses. However, except asking Sir George Wood whose troop it was, his Grace never even bestowed a regard on me as I followed from sub-division to sub-division."

The troop, as Mercer's story shows, was literally smashed up at Waterloo; but Mercer, with great energy and skill, quickly built it up again, and at a great review in Paris, where the allied sovereigns were present, the English guns were once more the admired of all observers. He writes:-

"It seems that we have been the rara avis of the day ever since our review. The rapidity of our movements, close-wheeling, perfection of our equipment, &c., &c., excited universal astonishment and admiration. The consequence of this was an application to the Duke for a closer inspection, which he most magnanimously granted, and ordered Ross's troop out for that purpose. They paraded in the fields near Clichy. The reviewers, I understand, were marechaux de France; but there was also a great concourse of officers of all nations. After the manoeuvres the troop was dismounted, and a most deliberate inspection or ammunition, and even of the men's kits, appointments, shoeing, construction of carriages, &c., &c., took place. I believe they were equally astonished and pleased with what they saw, and as there were several among them taking notes, have no doubt that we shall soon see improvements introduced into the Continental artillery."

Mercer, curiously enough, declares that the British artilleryman of his day had no affection for his horse, and in this respect compares very ill with the German artilleryman; the same thing, he says, applies to British and German cavalry:-

"Affection for, and care of, his horse is the trait par excellence which distinguishes the German dragoon from the English. The former would sell everything to feed his horse ; the latter would sell his horse itself for spirits, or the means of obtaining them. The one never thinks of himself until his horse is provided for; the other looks upon the animal as a curse and a source of perpetual drudgery to himself, and gives himself no concern about it when once away from under his officer's eye. The German accustoms his horse to partake of his own fare. I remember a beautiful mare, belonging to a sergeant of the 3rd Hussars, K.G.L., which would even eat onions. She was one of the very few that escaped after the disastrous retreat of Corunna, and had been saved and smuggled on board ship by the sergeant himself. In the Peninsula the only means of enforcing some attention to their horses amongst our English regiments was to make every man walk and carry his saddle-bags whose horse died or was ill."

All branches of the British army, it may be added, did not impress the allied sovereigns in the same favourable manner as the artillery. The British infantry seemed undersized as compared with Austrians, Prussians, &c. Mercer's account of the memorable review, held only five weeks after Waterloo, is interesting:-

"At length the approach of the sovereigns was announced, and they came preceded and followed by a most numerous and brilliant cortege, in which figured, perhaps, some of almost every arm of every army in Europe. It was a splendid and most interesting sight. First came the Emperor Alexander and the King of Prussia, in their respective green and blue uniforms, riding together the former, as usual, all smiles ; the latter taciturn and melancholy. A little in their rear followed the Austrian Emperor, in a white uniform, turned up with red, but quite plain a thin, dried-up, thread-paper of a man, not of the most distinguished bearing ; his lean, brown visage, however, bore an expression of kindness and bonhomie, which folk say his true character in no way belies. They passed along, scanning our people with evident interest and curiosity ; and in passing me (as they did to every commanding officer), pulled off their hats, and saluted me with most gracious smiles. I wonder if they do the same to their own. Until yesterday I had not seen any British infantry under arms since the evening the troops from America arrived at Garges, and, in the meantime, have constantly seen corps of foreign infantry.

"These are all uncommonly well dressed in new clothes, smartly made, setting the men off to the greatest advantage add to which their coiffure of high broad-topped shakos, or enormous caps of bearskin. Our infantry indeed our whole army appeared at the review in the same clothes in which they had marched, slept, and fought for months. The colour had faded to a dusky brick-dust hue ; their coats, originally not very smartly made, had acquired by constant wearing that loose, easy set so characteristic of old clothes, comfortable to the wearer, but not calculated to add grace to his appearance. Pour surcroit de laideur, their cap is perhaps the meanest, ugliest thing ever invented. From all these causes it arose that our infantry appeared to the utmost disadvantage dirty, shabby, mean, and very small. Some such impression was, I fear, made on the sovereigns, for a report has reached us this morning that they remarked to the Duke what very small men the English were. 'Ay,' replied our noble chief, 'they are small; but your Majesties will find none who fight so well.' I wonder if this is true. However small our men and mean their appearance, yet it was evident that they were objects of intense interest from the immense time and close scrutiny of the inspection."

THE FIELD OF WATERLOO

Mercer, with his troop, embarked at Harwich on April 9, and landed at Ostend on the 13th. Thence he marched, with frequent halts, to Brussels. His account of the marches and experiences of his troop is very interesting, if only as showing that even under a great commander like Wellington, amazing blunders and much distracted confusion were possible. Nothing more absurd can well be imagined than the fashion in which Mercer's fine troop was disembarked at Ostend; and nothing could be more planless and belated than the marching or rather the loitering of troop G towards Brussels. Wellington used to complain afterwards that in the Waterloo campaign he had the most villainous staff with which an unhappy general was ever afflicted; and the helpless quality of Wellington's staff is reflected in Mercer's account of the orders he received or did not receive directing his march to the front. Here is Mercer's account of how his troops started from their English barracks on the march which was to end on the smoky ridge at Waterloo:-

"On the morning of the 9th, the troop paraded at half-past seven o'clock

THE CHATEAU OF HOUGOUMONT

with as much regularity and as quietly as if only going to a field-day; not a man either absent or intoxicated, and every part of the guns and appointments in the most perfect order. At eight, the - hour named in orders, we marched off the parade. The weather was fine, the scenery, as we skirted the beautiful banks of the Stour, charming, and the occasion exhilarating. Near Manningtree we halted a short time to feed our horses, and then, pursuing our route, arrived at Harwich about three o'clock in the afternoon. Here we found the transports the Adventure, Philarea, and Solus, in which last I embarked.

"About 2 P.M. on the 11th, a light breeze from the N.W. induced our agent to get under way, and we repaired on board our respective ships with every prospect of a good and speedy passage. In this, however, we were disappointed, for the breeze dying away as the sun went down, we anchored, by signal, at the harbour's mouth, just as it got dark.

"The evening was splendid. A clear sky studded with myriads of stars overhead, and below a calm un- ruffled sea, reflecting on its glassy surface the lights of the distant town, the low murmuring sounds from which, and the rippling of the water under the ships' bows, were the only interruptions to the solemn stillness that prevailed after the people had retired to their berths. In our more immediate neighbourhood stretched out the long, low, sandy tract, on the seaward extremity of which the dark masses and Landguard fort could just be distinguished.

"With daybreak on the morning of the 12th came a favourable wind, though light, and again we took up our anchors and proceeded to sea. For some distance after clearing the harbour our course lay along the Suffolk coast, and so near in that objects on shore were plainly discernible. To us who had long been stationed at Woodbridge, only a few miles inland, this was highly interesting. We knew every village, every copse, every knoll nay, almost every tree. There were the houses in which we had so oft been hospitably entertained; there were the sheep-walks on which we had so often manoeuvred; and there in the distance, as we passed the mouth of the Deben, our glasses showed us the very barrack on the hill, with its tiled roofs illumined by the noontide sun. About Bawdsey we left the coast, and steered straight over with a light but favourable wind; the low, sandy shores of Suffolk soon sank beneath the horizon.

"During the night a light breeze right aft and smooth water enabled us to make good progress; but towards morning (13th) the wind had very considerably increased, and although the coast was not in sight, we were sensible of its neighbourhood from the number of curious heavy-looking boats plying round us in all directions, having the foremast with its huge lug-sail stuck right up in the bow or rather inclining over it.

"Nothing, certainly, could be more repulsive than the appearance of the coast sandhills as far as the eye could reach, broken only by the grey and lugubrious works and buildings of Ostend, and further west by the spires of Mittelkerke and Nieuport peering above the sandhills. The day, too, was one little calculated to enliven the scene. A fresh breeze and cloudy sky; the sea black, rough, and chilly; the land all under one uniform cold grey tint, presenting scarcely any relief of light and shadow, consequently no feature. Upon reconnoitring it, however, closer, we found that this forbidding exterior was only an outer coating to a lovely gem. Through the openings between the sand- hills could be seen a rich level country of the liveliest verdure, studded with villages and farms interspersed amongst avenues of trees and small patches of wood.

"A black-looking mass of timber rising from the waters off the entrance of the harbour, and which we understood to be a fort, now became the principal object of our attention. The harbour of Ostend is an artificial one, formed by jetees of piles projecting as far as low-water mark. The right on entering is merely a row of piles running along in front of the works of the town; but on the left is a long mole or jetee on the extremity of which is a small fort. Behind this mole to the north-"east the shore curving inwards forms a bight, presenting an extent of flat sandy beach on which the water is never more than a few feet deep even at the highest tides. A tremendous surf breaks on this whenever it blows from the westward.

"Followed by a crowd of other craft of all sorts and sizes, we shot rapidly along towards that part of the harbour where a dense assemblage of shipping filled up its whole breadth and forbade further progress, so that one wondered what was to become of the numerous vessels in our wake. The mystery was soon explained, for each having attained the point, turning her prow to the town, ran bump on the sands and there stuck fast. Those immediately above us had just arrived, and from them a regiment of Light Dragoons was in the act of disembarking, by throwing their horses overboard and then hauling them ashore by a long rope attached to their head-collars. What a scene! What hallooing, shouting, vociferating, and plunging! The poor horses did not appear much gratified by their sudden transition from the warm hold to a cold bath.

"Our keel had scarcely touched the sand ere we were abruptly boarded by

"BEFORE WATERLOO"
The Duchess of Richmond's famous ball on the eve of the battle of Waterloo
Henry Nelson O'Neil (1868)

a naval officer (Captain Hill) with a gang of sailors, who, sans ceremonie, instantly commenced hoisting our horses out, and throwing them, as well as our saddlery, &c., overboard, without ever giving time for making any disposition to receive or secure the one or the other. To my remonstrance his answer was, 'I can't help it, sir; the Duke's orders are positive that no delay is to take place in landing the troops as they arrive, and the ships sent back again ; so you must be out of her before dark.' It was then about 3 P.M., and I thought this a most uncomfortable arrangement.

"The scramble and confusion that ensued baffle all description. Bundles of harness went over the side in rapid succession as well as horses. In vain we urged the loss and damage that must accrue from such a proceeding. 'Can't help it no business of mine- Duke's orders are positive,' &c., &c., was our only answer. Meantime the ebb had begun to diminish the depth of water alongside, and enabled us to send parties overboard and to the beach to collect and carry our things ashore, as well as to haul and secure the horses. The same operation commenced from the other vessels as they arrived, and the bustle and noise were inconceivable. The dragoons and our men (some nearly, others quite, naked) were dashing in and out of the water, struggling with the affrighted horses, or securing their wet accoutrements as best they could. Some of the former were saddling their dripping horses, and others mounting and marching off in small parties. Disconsolate-looking groups of women and children were to be seen here and there sitting on their poor duds,

ARTILLERY AT THE BATTLE OF WATERLOO
George Jones (1786-1869)

or roaming about in search of their husbands, or mayhap of a stray child, all clamouring, lamenting, and materially increasing the babel-like confusion.

"It was not without difficulty that I succeeded at last in impressing upon Captain Hill the necessity of leaving our guns and ammunition-waggons, &c., on board for the night otherwise his furious zeal would have turned all out to stand on the wet sand or be washed away. Meantime, although we were on shore, we were without orders what to do next. Not an officer, either of the staff, the garrison, or even of our own corps, came near us. Night approached, and with it bad weather evidently. Our poor shivering horses and heaps of wet harness could not remain on the sands much longer, when the flood began to make again ; and it was necessary to look about and see what could be done. With this intent, therefore, leaving the officers to collect their divisions, I got one of my horses saddled and rode into the town. Here was the same bustle (although not the same confusion) as on the sands. The streets were thronged with British officers, and the quays with guns, waggons, horses, baggage, &c.

"One would hardly expect to meet with any delay in finding the commandant of a fortress, yet such was my case; and it was not until after long and repeated inquiry that I discovered Lieut.-Colonel Gregory, 44th Regiment, to be that personage, and found his residence. From him, however, I could obtain nothing. He seemed hardly to have expected the compliment of reporting our arrival, and stated that he had no other orders but that the troops of every arm should march for Ghent the moment they landed, without halting a single day in Ostend.

"Strange to say neither I nor the colonel recollected there was such a person in Ostend as an assistant- quarter-master-general, who should be referred to on such an occasion. Yet this was the case; and that officer, instead of attending to the debarkation of the troops, or making himself acquainted with the arrivals, kept out of sight altogether. Baffled at all points, I was returning to the sands when I met Major Druinmond on the Quai Imperial, and related my story. His advice was to march to Ghystelle (a village about six miles from Ostend), and after putting up there for the night, to return and disembark my guns, &c., in the morning. While speaking, however, some one (I forget who) came up with the agreeable information that Ghystelle was already fully occupied by the 16th Dragoons. He, however, gave me directions for some large sheds about a mile off, where his own horses had passed the preceding night.

"This was some consolation: so riding off immediately to reconnoitre the place and the road to it, I returned to the beach just as it got dark; and a most miserable scene of confusion I there found. Our saddles, harness, baggage, &c., were still strewed about the sand, and these the flood, which was now making, threatened soon to submerge. Pour surcroit de malheur, the rain came down in torrents, and a storm, which had been brewing up the whole afternoon, now burst over us most furiously. The lightning was quite tremendous, whilst a hurricane, howling horribly through the rigging of the ships, was only exceeded in noise by the loud explosions and rattling of the incessant claps of thunder.

"Our people, meantime, blinded by the lightning, had borrowed some lanterns from the ship, and were busily employed searching for the numerous articles still missing." The obscurity, however, between the vivid flashes was such that we were only enabled to keep together by repeatedly calling to each other, and it was not without difficulty and great watchfulness that we escaped being caught by the tide, which flowed rapidly in over the flat sands. At length, having collected as many of our things as was possible, and saddled our horses (some two or three of which had escaped altogether), we began our march for the sheds a little after midnight, with a farrier and another dismounted man carrying lanterns at the head of our column.

"The rain continued pouring, but flashes of lightning occurred now only at intervals, and the more subdued rolling of the thunder told us that it was passing away in the distance. Our route lay through the town, to gain which we found some advanced ditch to be crossed by a very frail wooden bridge. Half the column, perhaps, might have cleared this, when, 'crack,' down it went, precipitating all who were on it at the moment into the mud below, and completely cutting off those in the rear. Here was a dilemma. Ignorant of the localities, and without a guide, how was the rear of the column to join us, or how were the people in the ditch, with their horses, to be extricated? Luckily none were hurt seriously, and the depth was not great not more, perhaps, than six or eight feet; but that was enough to baffle all our attempts at extricating the horses. Some Belgic soldiers of a neighbouring guard, of which we were not aware, fortunately heard us, and came to our assistance ; and one of them, crossing the ditch, undertook to guide the rear of our column and those below to another gate, whilst one accompanied us to the Quai Imperial, where, after waiting a while, we were at length assembled, drenched with rain and starving of cold and hunger.

"The Quai was silent and dark; the only light gleamed dimly through the wet from a miserable lamp over the door of a cafe, in which people were still moving; and the only sounds that broke the stillness of the quarter were the splashing of the rain and the clattering of our steel scabbards and horses' feet

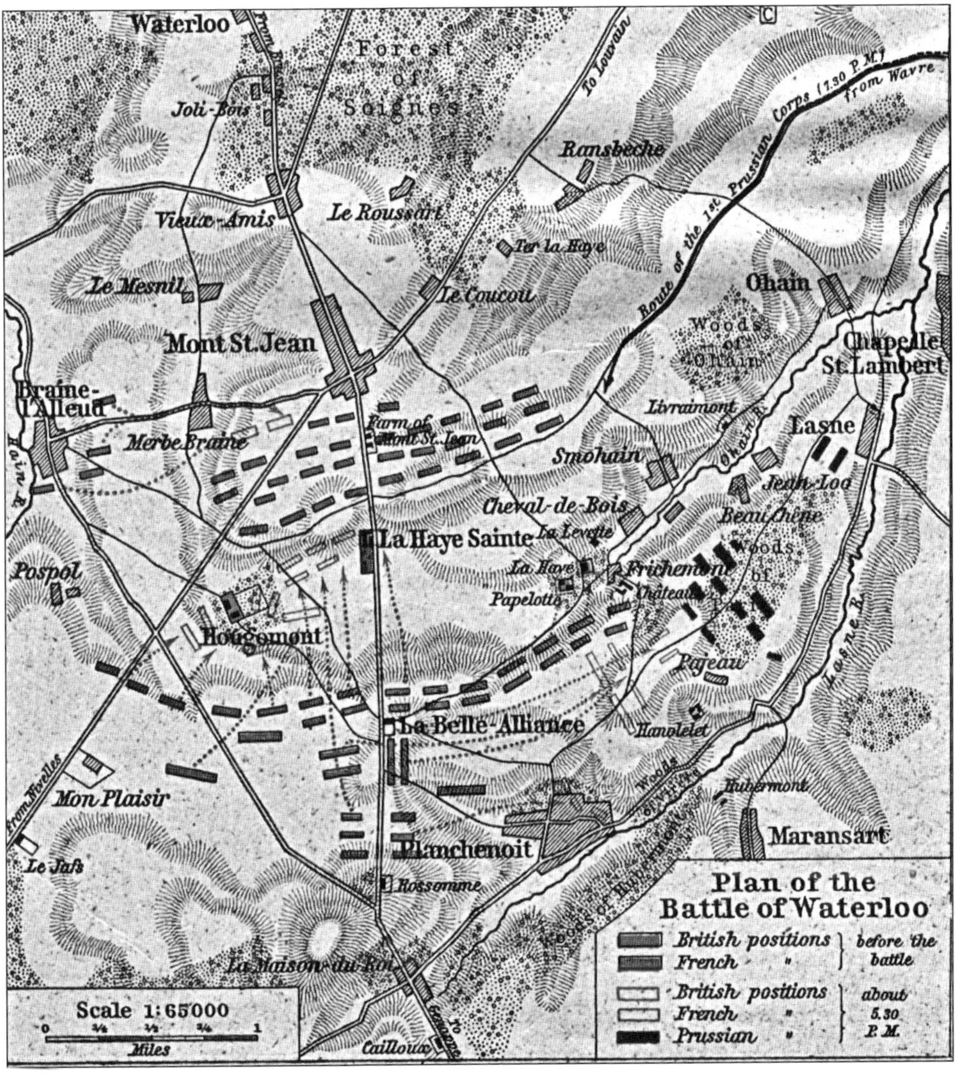

PLAN OF THE BATTLE OF WATERLOO

as we moved dejectedly on winding our way through un- known avenues (for in the dark I found it impossible to recognise the narrow streets through which I had so hurriedly passed in the afternoon), occasionally illuminated by a solitary lamp, the feeble light of which, however, was somewhat increased by reflection on the wet pavement. After following for some time this devious course, I began to fear I had missed the road, when again we stumbled upon a Belgic guard, by whose direction and guidance we at length reached the outer barrier. Here we again came to a standstill, the officer in charge refusing to let us out. Some altercation ensued; I forget the particulars, but it ended in his opening the gate.

"Once clear of the town, we hoped soon to reach our lodging; but had scarcely advanced a hundred yards ere we found that result was more distant than we had fancied, and that patience was still requisite. The rain had rendered the fat soil so slippery that our horses could scarcely keep their legs, and the road running along the narrow summit of a dyke, with ditches on each side, rendered precaution and slow movement imperative. Every moment the fall of some horse impeded the column; our lanterns went out; and after wandering a considerable time, we at length ascertained, by knocking up the people at a house by the wayside, that we had overshot our mark, and it was not until two in the morning that we succeeded in finding the sheds. These were immensely long buildings attached to some saw-mills, for what use I know not, unless to store planks, &c., for they were now empty; but they were admirably adapted to our purpose, since we could range all our horses along one side, while the men occupied the other, in one of them. A quantity of hay, and some straw, left by our predecessors, was a valuable acquisition to man and beast under such circumstances. All our enjoyments are the effect of contrast. It would be considered miserable enough to be obliged to pass the night under such equivocal shelter as these sheds afforded, and that, too, in wet clothes; yet did we now, after twelve hours of harassing work and exposure to the weather, look upon them as palaces, and having cared for our poor beasts as far as circumstances would permit, proceeded to prepare for that repose so necessary and so longed for.

"Our road back to the town, now we had daylight, appeared very short, and having dried considerably, was not so slippery as last night. The gates were not yet opened when we arrived; a crowd of workmen of different kinds had already assembled and were waiting for admission, as were we, for a few

BATTLE OF WATERLOO 1815
William Sadler

minutes. At last they opened, and we proceeded to the harbour in search of our ship. The quais, beach, &c., were thronged as on the day before, and we added to the bustle in disembarking our guns and carriages, &c. This was completed by eleven o'clock, and we were ready to march forward ; but the commissariat detained us waiting the issue of our rations until 3 P.M. four mortal hours, considering our eagerness to get on and explore this new country, and the bore of being confined to one spot, since it was impossible to wander about the town, seeing that we could not calculate the moment when these gentry might find it convenient to supply us. Of our horses two were still missing, as were some saddle-bags and a number of smaller articles; and this is not to be wondered at when the scandalous manner in which they were thrown overboard, the badness of the weather, the darkness of the night, together with the ebbing and flowing of the tide, are taken into consideration.

"The appearance, too, of the troop was vexatious in the extreme. Our noble horses, yesterday morning so sleek and spirited, now stood with drooping heads and rough staring coats, plainly indicating the mischief they had sustained in being taken from a hot hold, plunged into cold water, and then exposed for more than seven hours on an open beach to such a tempest of wind and rain as that we experienced last night. Here was a practical illustration of the folly of grooming and pampering military horses, destined as they are to such exposures and privations. As for our men, they looked jaded, their clothes all soiled with mud and wet, the sabres rusty, and the bearskins of their helmets flattened down by the rain. Still, however, they displayed the same spirit and alacrity as that which has always been a characteristic of the horse-artillery, more particularly of G troop."

The tedium of waiting for so many hours on Ostend beach was relieved by a naval incident of an exciting quality:-

"A loud cry of dismay suddenly pervaded the crowd, and all simultaneously rushed to the ramparts. I followed this movement. The morning, though somewhat overcast, had been fine, and the wind moderate; but as the day advanced, and the flood-tide set in, the south-westerly breeze had gradually increased to a gale. On reaching the rampart, I immediately observed that the flat shore to the northward, as far as the eye could reach, was covered with a sheet of white foam from the tremendous surf breaking on it; whilst the spray, rising in clouds and borne along before the blast, involved the whole neighbourhood in a thick salt mist. Nothing could be more savage and wild than the appearance of the coast.

"In the offing, numerous vessels under small sail were running for the harbour. One small brig had missed, and before assistance could be given, had been whirled round the jetee, and cast broadside on amongst the breakers. Her situation was truly awful. The surf broke over her in a frightful manner, sending its spray higher than her masts, and causing

BATTLE OF WATERLOO 1815
Thomas Jones Barker

GEBHARD LEBERECHT VON BLÜCHER
Blücher led one of the coalition armies defeating Napoleon at the Battle of Leipzig, and commanded the Prussian army

her to roll from side to side until her yards dipped in the water, and induced a belief every moment that she must roll over. Every now and then a huge wave, larger than its predecessor, would raise her bodily, and then, rapidly re- ceding, suddenly let her fall again on the ground with a concussion that made the masts bend and vibrate like fishing-rods, and seemed to threaten instant annihilation. Of her sails, some were torn to rags, and others, flying loose, flapped and fluttered with a noise that was audible from the rampart, despite the roaring of the surf. The people on board appeared in great agitation, and kept shouting to those on shore for assistance, which they were unable to give.

"Intense anxiety pervaded the assembled multitude as the shattered vessel alternately rose to view or was buried in a sea of foam. Numbers ran down to the sands opposite to her; and from them she could not have been twenty yards distant, yet could they not afford the despairing crew the slightest aid. Whilst thus attending in breathless expectation the horrid catastrophe, the return of our quarter-master with the rations summoned us unwillingly from the rampart to commence our march. We afterwards learnt that a boat from the harbour had succeeded in saving the crew (she had no troops on board) ; but the unfortunate pilot who thus gallantly risked his own life for them was killed by the boat rising suddenly under the vessel's counter as he stood in the bow, which dashed his brains out."

CHAPTER II

ON MARCH TO THE FIELD

Mercer's description of his march across the Low Countries is full of keen observation, and rich in pictures of peasant life. At Ghent the troop halted for seven days. Here the much-wandering Louis XVIII. held his Court, and Mercer gives an entertaining account of the scenes he witnessed:-

"During the seven days we remained in Ghent our time was so occupied by duties that there was little leisure to look about us. Amongst other duties, it fell to our lot to furnish a guard of honour to Louis XVIII., then residing in Ghent, his own troops having been sent to Alost to make room for the British, which were continually passing through. Our subalterns were very well pleased with this arrangement, for the duty was nothing. They found an excellent table, and passed their tune very agreeably with the young men of the gardes du corps, some of whom were always in attendance. Many of these were mere boys, and the ante-room of his most Christian Majesty frequently exhibited bolstering matches and other amusements, savouring strongly of the boarding-school. However, they were good-natured, and always most attentive to the comforts of the officer on guard. The royal stud was in the barrack stables, and consisted principally of grey horses, eighteen or twenty of which had been purchased in England at a sale of 'cast horses' from the Scots Greys.

"We frequently met French officers of all ranks, and formed acquaintance with many gentlemanly, well-informed men. At the Lion d'Or and Hotel de Flandre we found there was a table d'hote every night at eight o'clock, and, by way of passing the evening, usually resorted to one or the other for supper. Here we were sure of meeting many Frenchmen, and as the same people were generally constant attendants, we became intimate, and discussed the merits of our national troops respectively over our wine or ponche. It was the first time most of them had had an opportunity of inspecting British troops closely, though many had often met them in the field; and they were very curious in their inquiries into the organisation, government, and equipment of our army. Although allowing all due credit to the bravery displayed by our troops in the Peninsula, and the talents of our general (the Duke), yet were they unanimous in their belief that neither would avail in the approaching conflict, and that we must succumb before their idol and his grand army, for though these gentlemen had deserted Napoleon to follow the fortunes of Louis XVIII., it was evident they still revered the former.

WELLINGTON AND BLUCHER MEETING
BEFORE THE BATTLE OF WATERLOO
Robert Alexander Hillingford

"Their admiration of our troops, particularly of the cavalry, was very great, but they expressed astonishment at seeing so few decorations. It was in vain we asserted that medals were rarely given in the British army, and then only to commanding officers, &c. They shook their heads, appeared incredulous, and asked, 'Where are the troops that fought in Spain?' There might have been something more than mere curiosity in all this; there might have been an anxiety to ascertain whether their countrymen were about to cope with veterans or young soldiers. It might have been thrown out as a lure to provoke information relative to the present employment of those veteran bands. Moreover, I shrewdly suspected many of the gentlemen were actually spies.

"Amongst others who had followed Louis XVIII was Marmont. I think it was the day after our arrival, passing over the open space near the Place d'Armes by the river, I saw a French general officer exercising a horse in the manage, and learnt with astonishment that this was Marmont; for the man in question had two good arms, whereas for years past I had, in common with most people in England, looked upon it as a fact that he had left one at Salamanca. French deserters, both officers and privates, were daily coming in; it was said they deserted by hundreds."

On April 24 the troop received orders to resume its march, its next quarters being at Thermonde, or, as it ought to have been spelt, Dendermonde. From Dendermonde, on May 1, the troop was ordered to march to Strytem. Mercer had neither map, nor directions, nor guides, and his account of the incidents of the march, and the fashion in which (as though he were exploring some absolutely unknown land) he had to 'discover' Strytem is amusing:-

"May 1. - I still slept, when at five o'clock in the morning our sergeant-major aroused me to read a note brought by an orderly hussar. It was most laconic la void: 'Captain Mercer's troop of horse artillery will march to Strytem without delay. Signed,' &c., &c.

"Where is Strytem? And for what this sudden move? These were questions to which I could get no answer. The hussar knew nothing, and the people about me less. One thing was positive, and that was that we must be under way instantly, and pick out Strytem as best we might. The sergeant-major, therefore, was despatched to give the alert; and having given the hussar a receipt in full for his important despatch, I proceeded to clothe my person for the journey, having hitherto been en chemise. As the trumpeter was lodged in a house close by with my own grooms, the 'boot and saddle' quickly reverberated through the village, and set its whole population in movement.

"To my questions respecting Strytem, Monsieur could give no satisfactory

THE BATTLE OF WATERLOO
Ernest Crofts

answers. 'It lay in a very fine country somewhere in the neighbourhood of Brussels, and we had better take the road to that city in the first instance, and trust for further information to the peasantry as we went along.' These people are singularly ignorant in this respect, having no knowledge, generally speaking, of any place more than two or three miles from f home. Monsieur, however, invited me to follow him to his study a small room all in a litter over the gateway, and there, after some hunting amongst books, old clothes, &c., &c., he rummaged out the mutilated fragment of an old but very excellent map, which he insisted on my putting into my sabretache, which I did, and still keep for his sake.

"'Prepare to mount!' 'Mount!' The trumpets sound a march, and waving a last adieu to the group at the gate of my late home, I turn my back on it for ever perhaps. The men were in high spirits, and horses fat as pigs and sleek as moles thanks to rest, good stabling, and abundance of fodder. Most of the peasants on whom many of our men had been billeted accompanied them to the parade, and it was interesting to witness the kindness with which they shook hands at parting, and the complacency with which, patting the horses on the neck, they scanned them all over, as if proud of their good condition.

"Passing through Lebbeke, we found the three brigades of 9-pounders also getting on march, and the whole village astir. The officers told us their orders were to march direct to Brussels, and they were fully persuaded the French army had advanced.

"At Assche we found a battery of Belgian horse artillery in quarters. Then men lounging about in undress, or without their jackets, without any appearance of a move, induced us to believe our own was, after all, only another change of quarters and we were right. The people here knew Strytem, which they said was only a few miles distant, to the southward of the road we were on. Accordingly I despatched an officer to precede us, and make the necessary arrangements for our reception; at the same time, quitting the chaussee, we plunged into a villainous cross-road, all up and down, and every bottom occupied by a stream crossed by bridges of loose planks, which to us were rather annoying, from their apparent insecurity, as well as from the boggy state of the ground for some yards at either end of them.

"The road became worse than ever - deep, tenacious mud, sadly broken up. After marching a short distance we passed a wheelwright's shop ; then came to a broader space, where stood a small mean-looking church, a miserable cabaret, a forge, two very large farm establishments, with a few wretched-looking cottages this our guide gave us to understand was Strytem."

At Strytem, where the troop halted for some time, Mercer had an opportunity of seeing something of the cavalry corps which the Due de Bern was forming in the Bourbon interest. The Due de Berri, according to Mercer, was a very ill-mannered brute. Says Mercer:-

"One day I had a good opportunity of seeing this curious corps and its savage leader. The former presented a most grotesque appearance - cuirassiers, hussars, grenadiers a cheval, and chasseurs, dragoons and lancers, officers and privates, with a few of the new gardes du corps, were indiscriminately mingled in the ranks. One file were colonels, the next privates, and so on, and all wearing their proper uniforms and mounted on their proper horses, so that these were of all sizes and colours. There might have been about two hundred men, divided into two or three squadrons, the commanders of which were generals. The Prince, as I have said, was drill-master. A more intemperate, brutal, and (in his situation) impolitic one, can scarcely be conceived. The slightest fault (frequently occasioned by his own

THE BATTLE OF WATERLOO, 18 JUNE 1815 (1852)
Clément-Auguste Andrieux (1829–1880)

blunders) was visited by showers of low-life abuse using on all occasions the most odious language.

"One unfortunate squadron officer (a general!) offended him, and was immediately charged with such violence that I expected a catastrophe. Reining up his horse, however, close to the unhappy man, his vociferation and villainous abuse were those of a perfect madman; shaking his sabre at him, and even at one time thrusting the pommel of it into his face, and, as far as I could see, pushing it against his nose! Such a scene! Yet all the others sat mute as mice, and witnessed all this humiliation of their comrade, and the degradation of him for whom they had forsaken Napoleon. Just at this moment one of our troop-dogs ran barking at the heels of the Prince's horse. Boiling with rage before, he now boiled over in earnest, and, stooping, made a furious cut at the dog, which, eluding the weapon, continued his annoyance. The Duke, quitting the unfortunate chef d'escadron, now turned seriously at the dog, but he, accustomed to horses, kept circling about, yapping and snapping, and always out of reach; and it was not until he had tired himself

THE DECISIVE CHARGE OF THE LIFE GUARDS AT THE BATTLE OF WATERLOO
From the picture by Luke Clennel. Published by the London Illustrated News

with the fruitless pursuit that, foaming with rage, he returned to his doomed squadrons, who had sat quietly looking on at this exhibition."

As the early days of June passed, and Napoleon was preparing for his daring leap on the allied forces, the general strain grew more tense. French spies were busy all through the English and Prussian posts. Mercer describes a visit paid by a particularly daring spy to his own post:-

"It was on the evening of the 15th June, and about sunset or a little later, that an officer of hussars rode into the village of Yseringen, Leathes being at the time at dinner with me at our chateau. He was dressed as our hussars usually were when riding about the country blue frock, scarlet waistcoat laced with gold, pantaloons, and forage-cap of the 7th Hussars. He was mounted on a smart pony, with plain saddle and bridle; was without a sword or sash, and carried a small whip - in short, his costume and monture were correct in every particular. Moreover, he aped to the very life that 'devil-may-care' nonchalant air so frequently characterising our young men of fashion. Seeing some of our gunners standing at the door of a house, he desired them to go for their officer, as he wished to see him. They called the sergeant, who told him that the officer was not in the village.

"In an authoritative tone he then demanded how many men and horses were quartered there, whose troop they belonged to, where the remainder of the troop was quartered, and of what it consisted? When all these questions were answered, he told the sergeant that he had been sent by Lord Uxbridge to order accommodation to be provided for two hundred horses, and that ours must consequently be put up as close as possible. The sergeant replied that there was not room in the village for a single additional horse. 'Oh, well soon see that,' said he, pointing to one of the men who stood by, 'do you go and tell the maire to come instantly to me.' The maire came and confirmed the sergeant's statement, upon which our friend, flying into a passion, commenced his excellent French to abuse the poor functionary like a pickpocket, threatening to send a whole regiment into the village; and then, after a little further conversation with the sergeant, he mounted his pony and rode off just as Leathes returned to the village.

"Upon reporting the circumstances to the officer, the sergeant stated that he thought this man had appeared anxious to avoid him, having ridden off rather in a hurry when he appeared, which together with a slight foreign accent, then for the first time excited a suspicion of his being a spy, which had not occurred to the sergeant before, as he knew there were several foreign officers in our hussars, and that the loth was actually then commanded by one Colonel Quentin. The suspicion was afterwards confirmed, for upon inquiry, I found that no officer had been sent by Lord Uxbridge on any such mission. Our friend deserved to escape, for he was a bold and clever fellow."

QUATRE BRAS
Lady Elizabeth Butler

CHAPTER III
QUATRE BRAS

Napoleon's plan for what was to prove the last campaign in his own wonderful career was daring and subtle. He had to face two armies, each almost equal in strength to his own; and though the forces of Blucher and of Wellington were scattered over a very wide front, yet their outposts touched each other where the great road from Charleroi ran northwards to Brussels.

Napoleon, with equal audacity and genius, resolved to smite at the point of junction betwixt the two armies, and overthrow each in turn. The risks of this strategy were immense, for if his enemies succeeded in concentrating and fighting in concert, he would be overwhelmed and destroyed - as actually happened at Waterloo. Napoleon, however, calculated to win by the swiftness and suddenness of his stroke, destroying Blucher before Wellington could concentrate for his help, and then, in turn, overwhelming Wellington. By what a narrow interval that great plan failed of success is not always realised.

Both Blucher and Wellington were off their guard. On June 15, at the very moment when Napoleon's columns were crossing the Belgian frontier, Wellington was writing a leisurely despatch to the Czar explaining his intention to take the offensive at the end of the month. Blucher, only a few days before, as Houssaye records, had written to his wife, "We shall soon enter France. We might remain here another year, for Bonaparte will never attack us." Yet with miraculous energy and skill, Napoleon, in ten days, had gathered a host of 124,000 men, over distances ranging from 30 to 200 miles, and held them, almost unsuspected, within cannon-shot of the allied outposts. On June 15th, while the stars in the eastern summer sky were growing faint in the coming dawn, the French columns were crossing at three separate points the Belgian frontier, and the great campaign had begun.

Its history is compressed into three furious days. On the 16th Napoleon defeated Blucher at Ligny, while Wellington, with obstinate courage and fine skill, aided by many blunders on his enemy's part, and much good luck on his own, succeeded in holding Quatre Bras against Ney. On the 17th Wellington fell back before the combined armies of Napoleon and Ney to Waterloo. On the 18th the great battle, which sealed the fate of Napoleon and gave a long peace to Europe, was fought. Napoleon's strategy had fatally broken down. He aimed to separate the English and the Prussian armies while keeping his own concentrated. The exact opposite happened. Blucher's bold westward march from Wavre to Waterloo united the allied forces, while Napoleon's force was fatally divided - Grouchy, with 30,000 troops, being left "in the air" far to the east. Napoleon, in a word, suffered the exact strategic disaster he sought to inflict on his opponents.

We take up the thread of the adventures of Mercer and Battery G as active operations begin. It offers a curious picture of the distraction and confusion of a great campaign:-

"June 16. I was sound asleep when my servant, bustling into the room, awoke me en sursaut. He brought a note, which an orderly hussar had left and ridden off immediately. The note had nothing official in its appearance, and might have been an invitation to dinner; out the unceremonious manner in which the hussar had gone off without his receipt looked curious. My despatch was totally deficient in date, so that time and place were left to conjecture ; its contents pithy they were as follows, viz.:-

"'Captain Mercer's troop will proceed with the utmost diligence to Enghien, where he will meet Major M'Donald, who will point out the ground on which it is to bivouac to-night.

'Signed, D.A.Q.M.-Gen.'

"That we were to move forward, then, was certain. It was rather sudden, to be sure, and all the whys and wherefores were left to conjecture ; but the suddenness of it, and the importance of arriving quickly at the appointed place, rather alarmed me, for upon reflection I remembered that I had been guilty of two or three imprudences.

"First, all my officers were absent ; secondly, all my country waggons were absent ; thirdly, a whole division (one-third of my troop) was absent at Yseringen. 'Send the sergeant-major here,' was the first order, as I drew on my stockings. 'Send for Mr. Coates' (my commissariat officer), the second, as I got one leg into my overalls. 'William, make haste and get breakfast,' the third, as I buttoned them up. The sergeant-major soon came, and received his orders to turn out instanter, with the three days' provisions and forage in the haversacks and on the horses; also to send an express for the first division. He withdrew, and immediately the fine martial clang of 'boot and saddle' resounded through the village and courts of the chateau, making the woods ring again, and even the frogs stop to listen.

" The commissary soon made his appearance. 'What! are we off, sir?' 'Yes, without delay ; and you must collect your waggons as quickly as possible.' 'I fear, Captain Mercer, that will take some time, for St. Cyr's are gone to Ninove.' My folly here stared me full in the face. Mr. Coates said he

CHARGE OF THE FRENCH CUIRASSIERS AT WATERLOO
Henri Félix Emmanuel Philippoteaux

would do his utmost to collect them ; and as he was a most active, intelligent, and indefatigable fellow, I communicated to him my orders and determination not to wait, desiring him to follow us as soon as he possibly could. My first enumerated care was speedily removed, for I learned that the officers had just arrived and were preparing for the march, having known of it at Brussels ere we did. The two divisions in Strytem were ready to turn out in a few minutes after the 'boot and saddle' had resounded, but, as I feared, the first kept us waiting until near seven o'clock before it made its appearance. At length the first division arrived, and the animating and soul-stirring notes of the 'turn-out' again awoke the echoes of the hills and woods. Up jumped my old dog Bal, and away to parade and increase the bustle by jumping at the horses' noses and barking, as parade formed. Away went the officers to inspect their divisions, and Milward is leading my impatient charger, Cossac, up and down the court.

"We had cleared the village and marched some miles well enough, being within the range of my daily rides; but, this limit passed, I was immediately sensible of another error - that of having started without a guide; for the roads became so numerous, intricate, and bad, often resembling only woodmen's tracks, that I was sorely puzzled, spite of the map I carried in my sabretache, to pick out my way. But a graver error still I had now to reproach myself with, and one that might have been attended with fatal consequences. Eager to get on, and delayed by the badness of the roads, I left all my ammunition waggons behind, under charge of old Hall, my quartermaster-sergeant, to follow us, and then pushed on with the guns alone, thus foolishly enough dividing my troop into three columns - viz., the guns, ammunition waggons, and the column of provision waggons under the commissary. For this piece of folly I paid dearly in the anxiety I suffered throughout this eventful day, which at times was excessive.

"Rid of all encumbrances, we trotted merrily on whenever the road permitted, and, arriving at Castre (an old Roman legionary station), found there the 23rd Light Dragoons just turning out, having also received orders to march upon Enghien. A Captain Dance, with whom I rode a short distance, told me he had been at the ball at Brussels last night, and that, when he left the room, the report was that Blucher had been attacked in the morning, but that he had repulsed the enemy with great slaughter, was following up the blow, and that our advance was to support him. The road for the last few miles had been upon a more elevated country, not so wooded - a sort of plateau, consequently hard and dry ; but immediately on passing Castre, we came to a piece which appeared almost impassable for about a hundred yards a perfect black bog, across which a corduroy road had been made, but not kept in repair, consequently the logs, having decayed, left immense gaps.

"The 23rd floundered through this with difficulty, and left us behind. How we got through with our 9-pounders, the horses slipping up to the shoulders between the logs every minute, I know not ; but through we did get, and without accident, but it took time to do so. About noon, after threading our way through more mud and many watery lanes, doubtful if we were in the

THE MOMENT ENSIGN EWART CAPTURED THE FRENCH EAGLE DURING THE CAVALRY CHARGE OF THE ROYAL SCOTS GREYS AT THE BATTLE OF WATERLOO IN 1815.

SIR HENRY WILLIAM PAGET (1768-1854),
1ST MARQUESS OF ANGLESEY,
2ND EARL OF UXBRIDGE
Jan Willem Pieneman (1779-1853)

right direction, we came out upon a more open and dry country, close to a park, which upon inquiry proved to be that of Enghien. To the same point various columns of cavalry were converging, and under the park wall we found Sir Ormsby Vandeleur's brigade of light dragoons dismounted, and feeding their horses. Here we also dismounted to await the arrival of Major M'Donald; and as I looked upon the day's march as finished, deferred feeding until our bivouac should be established - another folly, for an officer in campaign should never lose an opportunity of feeding, watering, or resting his horses, &c. Having waited a good half-hour, and no Major M'Donald appearing, I began to look about for some one who could give me information, but no staff-officer was to be seen, and no one else knew anything about the matter. Corps after corps arrived and passed on, generally without even halting, yet all professing ignorance of their destination. Pleasant situation this!

"Sir Ormsby's dragoons were by this time bridling up their horses and rolling up their nosebags, evidently with the intention of moving off'. Seeing this, I sought out the general, whom I found seated against a bank that, instead of a hedge, bordered the road. Whether naturally a savage, or that he feared committing himself, I know not, but Sir Ormsby cut my queries short with an asperity totally uncalled for. 'I know nothing about you, sir! I know nothing at all about you!' 'But you, you already I know nothing at all about you and starting abruptly from his seat, my friend mounted his horse, and (I suppose by instinct) took the road towards Steenkerke, followed by his brigade, leaving me and mine alone in the road, more disagreeably situated than ever. I now began to reflect very seriously on the 'to stay' or 'not to stay.' In the former case, I bade fair to have the ground all to myself, for although everybody I spoke to denied having any orders, yet all kept moving in one and the same direction. In the latter case, my orders in writing certainly were to stay; but circumstances might have occurred since to change this, and the new order might not have reached me. Moreover, it was better to get into a scrape for fighting than keeping out of the way, so I made up my mind to move forward too.

"Accordingly I had already mounted my people when Sir H. Vivian's brigade of hussars, followed by Major Bull's troop of our horse artillery, passed. Bull, I found, was, like myself, without orders, but he thought it best to stick close to the cavalry, and advised me to do the same, which I did, following him and them on the road to Steenkerke. The country about this place appeared more bare and forbidding than any I had yet seen in the Pays Baa Just as we moved off, the column of Household troops made its appearance, advancing from Ninove, and taking the same direction.

"It was now that the recollection of my absent waggons began to torment me, and I actually feared never to see them again. However, there was no help for it now, and I continued onward. A few miles farther we crossed the Senne by an old stone bridge, and about four hi the afternoon arrived at Braine le Comte, almost ravenous with hunger, and roasted alive by the burning sun, under which we had been marching all day.

"We found several regiments drawn up in close columns, dismounted and feeding. It was somewhere between Enghien and Braine le Comte that we met an aide-de-camp (I believe one of the Duke's) posting away as fast as his poor tired beast could get along, and dressed in his embroidered suit, white pantaloons, &c., &c., having evidently mounted as he left the ballroom. This, I remember, struck us at the time as rather odd, but we had no idea of the real state of our affairs.

"We had formed up, and were feeding also, but the nosebags were scarcely put on the poor horse's heads than the cavalry corps, mounting again, moved off, one after the other, and we were constrained to follow ere the animals had half finished. Here, as before, I could obtain no intelligence respecting our march, the direction and meaning of which all I spoke to professed a profound ignorance. Whilst halting, Hitchins, slipping into the town, brought us out a couple of bottles of wine, the which we passed round from one to the other without any scruple about sucking it all out of one muzzle.

"A little hamlet (Long Tour, I think) lay at the foot of the hills, the straggling street of which we found so crowded with baggage-waggons of some Hanoverian or other foreign corps that for a long while we were unable to pass. The cavalry, therefore, left us behind, for they broke into the adjoining fields until they had cleared the impediment. Although annoyed at being thus hindered, I could not but admire the lightness, and even elegance, of the little waggons, with their neat white tilts, and as neat and pretty jungfrauen who were snugly seated under them. We found the ascent of the hills more difficult than we expected, the road, which went up in a zigzag (indeed, it could not have been otherwise), little better than a woodman's track, much cut up, and exceedingly steep - so much so, that we found it necessary to double-horse all our carriages by taking only half up at once."

Now, at last, the sullen guns from Quatre Bras began to make themselves audible. Mercer's gunners were chiefly recruits; they had never yet heard the deep, vibrating sounds that tell of the shock of mighty hosts. That far-off call of angry guns stirred their blood and quickened their march ; but the troop reached Quatre Bras only when the battle ended. Mercer's narrative, however, gives a striking picture of how a great battle affects everything within sound of its guns:-

"At length the whole of our carriages were on the summit, but we were now quite alone, all the cavalry having gone on; and thus we continued our march on an elevated plateau, still covered with forest, thicker and more gloomy than ever. At length we had crossed the forest, and found ourselves

HOUGEMONT - PROOF ENGRAVING PUBLISHED IN
'THE MISCELLANEOUS PROSE WORKS OF SIR WALTER SCOTT'
William Miller (1796–1882)

on the verge of a declivity which stretched away less abruptly than the one we had ascended, consequently presenting a more extensive slope, down which our road continued. A most extensive view lay before us; and now, for the first time, as emerging from the woods, we became sensible of a dull, sullen sound that filled the air, somewhat resembling that of a distant water-mill, or still more distant thunder. On clearing the wood it became more distinct, and its character was no longer questionable - heavy firing of cannon and musketry, which could now be distinguished from each other plainly. We could also hear the musketry in volleys and independent firing. The extensive view below us was bounded towards the horizon by a dark line of wood, above which, in the direction of the cannonade, volumes of grey smoke arose, leaving no doubt of what was going on. The object of our march was now evident, and we commenced descending the long slope with an animation we had not felt before.

"It was here that Major M'Donald overtook us, and without adverting to the bivouac at Enghien, of which probably he had never heard, gave me orders to attach myself to the Household Brigade, under Lord Edward Somerset, but no instructions where or when. I took care not to tell him they were in the rear, lest he might order us to halt for them, which would have been a sore punishment to people excited as we now were by the increasing roar of the battle evidently going on, and hoped that by marching faster they might soon overtake us. Just at this moment a cabriolet, driving at a smart pace, passed us. In it was seated an officer of the Guards, coat open and snuff-box in hand. I could not but admire the perfect nonchalance with which my man was thus hurrying forward to join in a bloody combat - much, perhaps, in the same manner, though certainly not in the same costume, as he might drive to Epsom or Ascot Heath. The descent terminated in a picturesque hollow, with a broad pool, dark and calm, and beyond it an old mill, perfectly in keeping with the scene. The opportunity of watering, our poor brutes was too good to be missed, and I accordingly ordered a halt for that purpose. Whilst so employed, an aide-de-camp, descending from a

THE CHARGE OF THE SCOTS GREYS
Lady Elizabeth Butler

singular knoll above us, on which I had noticed a group of officers looking out with their glasses in the direction of the battle, came to summon me to Sir Hussey Vivian, who was one of them.

"On ascending the knoll Sir Hussey called to me in a hurried manner to make haste. 'Who do you belong to?' said he. I told him, as also that the brigade was yet in the rear. 'Well,' he replied, 'never mind; there is something serious going on, to judge from that heavy firing, and artillery must be wanted; therefore bring up your guns as fast as you can, and join my hussars; can you keep up?' 'I hope so, sir.' 'Well, come along without delay; we must move smartly.' In a few minutes our people, guns and all, were on the hill. The hussars, mounted, set off at a brisk trot, and we followed. Alas ! thought I, where are my ammunition waggons? The hussars, to lighten their horses, untied the nets containing their hay, and the mouths of their corn-bags, which, falling from them as they trotted on, the road was soon covered with hay and oats. We did not follow their example, and although dragging with us 9-pounders preserved our forage and also our place in the column.

"By-and-by a large town appeared in front of us, and the increasing intensity of the cannonade and volumes of smoke about the trees led us to suppose the battle near at hand, and on the hill just beyond the town.

"This town was Nivelle.

"Beyond the town the ground rose, also in shadowy obscurity, crowned with sombre woods, over which ascended the greyish-blue smoke of the battle, now apparently so near that we fancied we could hear the shouts of the combatants - a fancy strengthened by crowds of people on the heights, whom we mistook for troops - inhabitants of Nivelle, as we soon discovered, seeking to get a sight of the fearful tragedy then enacting. Before entering the town we halted for a moment, lighted our slow matches, put shot into our leathern cartouches, loaded the guns with powder, and stuck priming wires into the vents to prevent the cartridges slipping forward, and, thus prepared for immediate action, again moved on.

"On entering the town what a scene presented itself! All was confusion, agitation, and movement. The danger was impending; explosion after explosion, startling from their vicinity, and clattering peals of musketry, like those lengthened thunder-claps which announce to us so awfully the immediate neighbourhood of the electric cloud. The whole population of Nivelle was in the streets, doors and windows all wide open, whilst the inmates of the houses, male and female, stood huddled together in little groups like frightened sheep, or were hurrying along with the distracted air of people uncertain where they are going or what they are doing. In a sort of square which we traversed a few soldiers, with the air of citizens, probably a municipal guard, were drawn up hi line, looking anxiously about them at the numerous bleeding figures which we now began to meet.

"Some were staggering along unaided, the blood falling from them in large drops as they went. One man we met was wounded in the head; pale and ghastly, with affrighted looks and uncertain step, he evidently knew little of where he was or what passed about him, though still he staggered forward, the blood streaming down his face on to the greatcoat which he wore rolled over his left shoulder. An anxious crowd was collecting round him as we passed on. Then came others supported between two comrades, their faces

THE PRINCE OF ORANGE AT QUATRE BRAS

deadly pale and knees yielding at every step. At every step, in short, we met numbers, more or less wounded, hurrying along in search of that assistance which many would never live to receive, and others receive too late. Priests were running to and fro, hastening to assist at the last moments of a dying man ; all were in haste - all wore that abstracted air so inseparable from those engaged in an absorbing pursuit. Many would run up, and, patting our horses' necks, would call down benedictions on us, and bid us hasten to the fight ere it were yet too late, or uttering trembling and not loud shouts of 'Vivent les Anglais!'

"A few there were who stood apart, with gloomy, discontented looks, eyeing their fellow-citizens with evident contempt and us with scowls, not unmixed with derision, as they marked our dusty and jaded appearance. Through all this crowd we held our way, and soon began to ascend the hill beyond the town, where we entered a fine chaussee bordered by elms, expecting every moment to enter on the field of action, the roar of which appeared quite close to us. It was, however, yet distant.

"The road was covered with soldiers, many of them wounded, but also many apparently untouched. The numbers thus leaving the field appeared extraordinary. Many of the wounded had six, eight, ten, and even more attendants. When questioned about the battle, and why they left it, the answer was invariable: 'Monsieur, tout est perdu! Les Anglais sont abimes, en deroute, abimes, tous, tous, tous!' and then, nothing abashed, these fellows would resume their hurried route. My countrymen will rejoice to learn that amongst this dastardly crew not one Briton appeared. Whether they were of Nassau or Belgians I know not; they were one or the other I think the latter.

"One redcoat we did meet - not a fugitive though, for he was severely wounded. This man was a private of the 92nd (Gordon Highlanders), a short, rough, hardy-looking fellow, with the national high cheek- bones, and a complexion that spoke of many a bivouac. He came limping along, evidently with difficulty and suffering. I stopped him to ask news of the battle, telling him what I had heard from the others, 'Na, na, sir, it's aw a damned lee; they war fechtin' yat an' I laft 'em; but it's a bludy business, and thar's na saying fat may be the end on't. Oor ragiment was nigh clean swapt-aff, and oor colonel kilt just as I cam' awa'. Upon inquiring about his own wound, we found that a musket ball had lodged in his knee, or near it; accordingly Hitchins, dismounting, seated him on the parapet of a little bridge we happened to be on, extracted the ball in a few minutes, and, binding up the wound, sent him hobbling along towards Nivelle, not having extracted a single exclamation from the poor man, who gratefully thanked him as he resumed his way.

"A little farther on, and as it began to grow dusk, we traversed the village of Hautain le Val, where a very different scene presented itself. Here, in a large cabaret by the roadside, we saw through the open windows the rooms filled with soldiers, cavalry and infantry; some standing about in earnest conversation, others seated around tables, smoking, carousing, and thumping the board with clenched fists, as they related with loud voices - what? - most likely their own gallant exploits. About the door their poor horses, tied to a rail, showed by their drooping heads, shifting legs, and the sweat drying and fuming on their soiled coats, that their exertions at least had been of no trivial nature.

ENGLISH HOUSEHOLD CAVALRY

"The firing began to grow slacker, and even intermitting, as we entered on the field of Quatre Bras - our horses stumbling from time to time over corpses of the slain, which they were too tired to step over. The shot and shell which flew over our line of march from time to time (some of the latter bursting beyond us) were sufficient to enable us to say we had been in the battle of Quatre Bras, for such was the name of the place where we now arrived, just too late to be useful. In all directions the busy hum of human voices was heard; the wood along the skirts of which we marched re-echoed clearly and loudly the tones of the bugle, which ever and anon were overpowered by the sullen roar of cannon, or the sharper rattle of musketry; dark crowds of men moved in the increasing obscurity of evening, and the whole scene seemed alive with them. What a moment of excitement and anxiety as we proceeded amongst all this tumult, and amidst the dead and dying, ignorant as yet how the affair had terminated! Arrived at a mass of buildings, where four roads met (les quatre bras), Major M'Donald again came up with orders for us to bivouac on an adjoining field, where, accordingly, we established ourselves amongst the remains of a wheat crop.

A BRITISH SQUARE AT WATERLOO PUTS UP DOGGED RESISTANCE AGAINST ATTACKING FRENCH CAVALRY.
Cassell's Illustrated History of England

"June 17 - A popping fire of musketry, apparently close at hand, aroused me again to consciousness of my situation. At first I could not imagine where I was. I looked straight up, and the stars were twinkling over me in a clear sky. I put out a hand from beneath my cloak, and felt clods of damp earth and stalks of straw. The rattle of musketry increased, and then the consciousness of my situation came gradually over me. Although somewhat chilly, I was still drowsy, and regardless of what might be going on, had turned on my side and began to doze again, when one of my neighbours started up with the exclamation, ' I wonder what all that firing means! 'This in an instant dispelled all desire to sleep; and up I got too, mechanically repeating his words, and rubbing my eyes as I began to peer about.

"One of the first, and certainly the most gratifying, sights that met my inquiring gaze, was Quartermaster Hall, who had arrived during the night with all his charge safe and sound. He had neither seen nor heard, however, of Mr. Coates and his train of country waggons, for whom I began now to entertain serious apprehensions. From whatever the musketry might proceed, we could see nothing - not even the flashes; but the increasing light allowed me to distinguish numberless dark forms on the ground all around me, people slumbering still, regardless of the firing that had aroused me. At a little distance numerous white discs, which were continually in motion, changing place and disappearing, to be succeeded by others, puzzled me exceedingly, and I could not even form a conjecture as to what they might be. Watching them attentively, I was still more surprised when some of these white objects ascended from the ground and suddenly disappeared; but the mystery was soon explained by the increasing light, which gave to my view a corps of Nassau troops lying on the ground, having white tops to their shakos.

"Daylight now gradually unfolded to us our situation. We were on a plateau which had been covered with corn, now almost everywhere trodden down. Four roads, as already mentioned, met a little to the right of our front, and just at that point stood a farmhouse, which, with its outbuildings, yard, &c., was enclosed by a very high wall. This was the farm of Quatre Bras. Beyond it, looking obliquely to the right, the wood (in which the battle still lingered when we arrived last night) stretched away some distance along the roads to Nivelle and Charleroi, which last we understood lay in front."

CHAPTER IV
THE RETREAT TO WATERLOO

Mercer's battery formed part of the British rear-guard in the retreat from Quatre Bras to Waterloo, and his gunners had some very breathless and exciting experiences on the road, with the thunder rolling over their heads and the French cavalry charging furiously on their rear. Mercer tells the story with great vividness and spirit:-

"On the Charleroi road and in the plain was a small village (Frasnes), with its church, just beyond which the road ascended the heights, on the open part of which, between the road and the wood towards the left, was the bivouac of the French army opposed to us. Its advanced posts were in the valley near Frasnes, and ours opposite to them - our main body occupying the ground between Quatre Bras and the wood on the left. A smart skirmish was going on amongst the hedges, &c., already mentioned, and this was the firing we had heard all the morning. Our infantry were lying about, cleaning their arms, cooking, or amusing themselves, totally regardless of the skirmish. This, however, from our position, was a very interesting sight to me, for the slope of the ground enabled me to see distinctly all the manoeuvres of both parties, as on a plan. After much tiring from the edge of the wood, opposite which our riflemen occupied all the hedges, I saw the French chasseurs suddenly make a rush forward in all directions, whilst the fire of our people became thicker and faster than ever. Many of the former scampered across the open fields until they reached the nearest hedges, whilst others ran crouching under cover of those perpendicular to their front, and the whole succeeded in establishing themselves - thus forcing back and gaining ground on our men.

"The fire then again became sharper than ever sometimes the French were driven back; and this alternation I watched with great interest until summoned to Major M'Donald, who brought us orders for the day. From him I first learned the result of the action of yesterday - the retreat of the Prussians, and that we were to do so too. His directions to me were that I should follow some corps of infantry, or something of the sort; for what followed caused me to forget it all: ' Major Ramsay's troop,' he said, 'will remain in the rear with the cavalry to cover the retreat ; but I will not conceal from you that it falls to your turn to do this, if you choose it.' The major looked rather conscience-stricken as he made this avowal, so, to relieve him, I begged he would give the devil his due and me mine. Accordingly all the others marched off, and as nothing was likely to take place immediately, we amused ourselves by looking on at what was doing.

"Just at this moment an amazing outcry arose amongst the infantry at the farm, who were running towards us in a confused mass, shouting and bellowing, jostling and pushing each other. I made sure the enemy's cavalry had made a dash amongst them, especially as the fire of the skirmishers became thicker and apparently nearer, when the thing was explained by a large pig, squealing as if already stuck, bursting from the throng by which he was beset in all directions. Some struck at him with axes, others with the butts of their muskets, others stabbed at him with bayonets. The chase would have been amusing had it not been so brutal; and I have seldom experienced greater horror than I did on this occasion, when the poor brute, staggering from the repeated blows he received, was at last brought to the ground by at least half-a-dozen bayonets plunged into him at once.

"All this time our retreat was going on very quietly. The corps at Quatre Bras had retired early in the morning, and been replaced by others from the left, and this continued constantly - every corps halting for a time on the ground near Quatre Bras until another from the left arrived, these moving off on the great road to Brussels, ceding the ground to the new-comers.

"At first every one, exulting in the success of yesterday - they having repulsed the enemy with a handful of men, as it were, unsupported by cavalry

STORMING OF THE VILLAGE OF PLANCENOIT DURING THE BATTLE OF WATERLOO
Ludwig Elsholtz (1805–1850)

and with very little artillery - anticipated, now our army was united nothing less than an immediate attack on the French position. We were sadly knocked down, then, when the certainty of our retreat became known. It was in vain we were told the retreat was only a manoeuvre of concentration; the most gloomy anticipations pervaded every breast. About this time Sir Alexander Dickson paid me a visit, having just arrived from New Orleans, where he commanded the artillery, to be our deputy- quartermaster-general. He only stayed a few minutes.

"As the infantry corps on the plateau became fewer, the fire of the skirmishers amongst the hedges gradually relaxed, and at length ceased - the Rifles, &c., being drawn, and following the line of retreat. At last, about noon, I found myself left with my troop, quite alone, on the brow of the position, just by the farm of Quatre Bras - the only troops in sight being a small picket of hussars, near the village of Frasnes, in the plain below ; a few more in our rear, but at some little distance, amongst the houses ; and a brigade of hussars far away to the left (about two miles), close to the wood hi that quarter. Thus solitary, as it were, I had ample leisure to contemplate the scene of desolation around me, so strangely at variance with the otherwise smiling landscape. Everywhere mementoes of yesterday's bloody struggle met the eye the - corn trampled down, and the ground, particularly in the plain, plentifully besprinkled with bodies of the slain. Just in front of the farm of Quatre Bras there was a fearful scene of slaughter - Highlanders and cuirassiers lying thickly strewn about; the latter appeared to have charged up the Charleroi road, on which, and immediately bordering it, they lay most numerously.

"In communicating to me the orders of our retreat, Major M'Donald had reiterated that to join Lord Edward Somerset's brigade without delay, but still he could not tell me where this brigade was to be found. Meantime Sir Ormsby Vandeleur's brigade of light dragoons having formed up in front of the houses, and supposing from this that all the cavalry must be nigh, as one step towards finding Lord Edward I crossed the road to the right of these dragoons, and rode towards the part where, as before stated, the light was intercepted by trees and bushes. On passing through these I had an uninterrupted view of the country for miles, but not a soldier or living being was to be seen in that direction. As I pushed on through the thickets my horse, suddenly coming to a stand, began to snort, and showed unequivocal symptoms of fear. I drove him on, however, but started myself when I saw, lying under the bush, the body of a. man stripped naked. This victim of war was a youth of fair form, skin delicately white, and face but little darker; an embryo moustache decorated the upper lip, and his countenance, even in death, was beautiful. That he was French I conjectured, but neither on himself nor his horse was there a particle of clothing that could indicate to what nation he belonged. If French, how came he here to die alone so far in the rear of our lines?

"I know not why, but the rencontre with this solitary corpse had a wonderful effect on my spirits - far different from what I felt when gazing on the heaps that encumbered the field beyond. Seldom have I experienced such despondency - such heart-sinking - as when standing over this handsome form thus despoiled, neglected, and about to become a prey to wolves and carrion crows - the darling of some fond mother, the adored of some fair maid. His horse, stripped like himself, lay by - they had met their fate at once. Returning to my troop, I found Sir Augustus Frazer, who had come to order my ammunition waggons to the rear that the retreat might be as little encumbered as possible, and to tell me that what ammunition was used during the day would be supplied by my sending for it to Langeveldt, on the road to Brussels, where that to Wavre branches from it.

"Thus divested of our ammunition, it was evident that our retreat must be a rapid one, since with only fifty rounds a gun (the number in the limbers), it could not be expected that we could occupy any position longer than a few minutes. In the end, this measure nearly led to very disagreeable results, as will be seen anon."

Lord Uxbridge - afterwards the Marquis of Anglesey - was a very fine cavalry leader, a sort of English Murat, with all the dash, activity, and resource of that famous soldier. But he had too much fire in his temper for cool generalship. The tumult and shock of battle had the effect of champagne upon him. It kindled in his brain a sort of intoxication. So he took risks a cooler- headed soldier would have avoided. Uxbridge's fiery and audacious daring is vividly reflected in Mercer's account of how he covered the retreat to Waterloo:-

"It was now about one o'clock. My battery stood in position on the brow of the declivity, with its right near the wall of the farm, all alone, the only

ATTACK ON PLANCENOIT.
The attack by Prussian Divisions of Hiller, Ryssel and Tippelskirch overwhelmed the French Imperial Young Guard and the 1st Battalions of the 2nd Grenadiers and 2nd Chasseurs.
Adolf Northern (1828 -1876)

troops in sight being, as before mentioned, the picket and a few scattered hussars in the direction of Frasnes, Sir O. Vandeleur's light dragoons two or three hundred yards in our rear, and Sir H. Vivian's hussars far away to the left. Still the French array made no demonstration of an advance. This inactivity was unaccountable. Lord Uxbridge and an aide-de-camp came to the front of my battery, and dismounting, seated himself on the ground; so did I and the aide-de-camp. His lordship with his glass was watching the French position ; and we were all three wondering at their want of observation and inactivity, which had not only permitted our infantry to retire unmolested, but also still retained them in their bivouac. 'It will not be long now before they are on us,' said the aide-de-camp, 'for they always dine before they move ; and those smokes seem to indicate that they are cooking now.'

"He was right; for not long afterwards another aide-de-camp, scouring along the valley, came to report that a heavy column of cavalry was advancing through the opening between the woods to the left from the direction of Gembloux. At the same moment we saw them distinctly; and Lord Uxbridge having reconnoitred them a moment through his glass, started up, exclaiming, in a joyful tone, 'By the Lord, they are Prussians!' jumped on his horse, and, followed by the two aides, dashed off like a whirlwind to meet them. For a moment I stood looking after them as they swept down the slope, and could not help wondering how the Prussians came there. I was, however, not left long in my perplexity, for, turning my eyes towards the French position, I saw their whole army descending from it in three or four dark masses, whilst their advanced cavalry picket was already skirmishing with and driving back our hussars. The truth instantly flashed on my mind, and I became exceedingly uneasy for the safety of Lord Uxbridge and his companions, now far advanced on their way down the valley, and likely to be irretrievably cut off.

"My situation now appeared somewhat awkward; left without orders and entirely alone on the brow of our position - the hussar pickets galloping in and hurrying past as fast as they could - the whole French army advancing, and already at no great distance. In this dilemma, I determined to retire across the little dip that separated me from Sir O. Vandeleur, and take up a position in front of his squadrons, whence, after giving a round to the French, advance as soon as they stood on- our present ground, I thought I could retire in sufficient time through his intervals to leave the ground clear for him to charge. This movement was immediately executed; but the guns were scarcely unlimbered ere Sir Ormsby came furiously up, exclaiming, 'What are you doing here, sir? You encumber my front, and we shall not be able to charge. Take your guns away, sir; instantly, I say - take them away!' It was in vain that I endeavoured to explain my intentions, and that our fire would allow his charge to be made with more effect. 'No, no; take them out of my way, sir! was all the answer I could get; and accordingly, I was pre- paring to obey, when up came Lord Uxbridge, and the scene changed in a twinkling.

'Captain Mercer, are you loaded?' 'Yes, my lord.' 'Then give them a round as they rise the hill, and retire as quickly as possible.' 'Light dragoons, threes right; at a trot, march!' and then some orders to Sir Ormsby, of whom I saw no more that day. "'They are just coming up the hill,' said Lord Uxbridge. 'Let them get well up before you fire. Do you think you can retire quick enough afterwards?' 'I am sure of it, my lord.' 'Very well, then, keep a good lookout, and point your guns well.'

"I had often longed to see Napoleon, that mighty man of war - that astonishing genius who had filled the world with his renown. Now I saw him, and there was a degree of sublimity in the interview rarely equalled.* The sky had become overcast since the morning, and at this moment presented a most extraordinary appearance. Large isolated masses of thunder-cloud, of the deepest, almost inky black, their lower edges hard and strongly defined, lagging down, as if momentarily about to burst, hung suspended over us, involving our position and everything on it in deep and gloomy obscurity; whilst the distant hill lately occupied by the French army still lay bathed in brilliant sunshine. Lord Uxbridge was yet speaking when a single horseman, immediately followed by several others, mounted the plateau I had left at a gallop, their dark figures thrown forward in strong relief from the illuminated distance, making them appear much nearer to us than they really were.

"For an instant they pulled up and regarded us, when several squadrons coming rapidly on the plateau, Lord Uxbridge cried out, 'Fire!-fire!' and, giving them a general discharge, we quickly limbered up to retire, as they dashed forward supported by some horse artillery guns, which opened upon us ere we could complete the manoeuvre, but without much effect, for the only one touched was the servant of Major Whinyates, who was wounded in the leg by the splinter of a howitzer shell.

"It was now for the first time that I discovered the major and his rocket-

** That this was Napoleon we have the authority of General Gourgaud, who states that, irritated at the delay of Marshal Ney, he put himself at the head of the chasseurs (I think), and dashed forward in the hope of yet being able to catch our rearguard.*

THE DEATH OF SIR THOMAS PICTON

troop, who, annoyed at my having the rear, had disobeyed the order to retreat, and remained somewhere in the neighbourhood until this moment, hoping to share whatever might be going on. The first gun that was fired seemed to burst the clouds overhead, for its report was instantly followed by an awful clap of thunder, and lightning that almost blinded us, whilst the rain came down as if a waterspout had broken over us. The sublimity of the scene was inconceivable. Flash succeeded flash, and the peals of thunder were long and tremendous; whilst, as if in mockery of the elements, the French guns still sent forth - their feebler glare and now scarcely audible reports their cavalry dashing on at a headlong pace, adding their shouts to the uproar. We galloped for our lives through the storm, striving to gain the enclosures about the houses of the hamlets, Lord Uxbridge urging us on, crying, 'Make haste! make haste! for God's sake, gallop, or you will be taken!' We did make haste, and succeeded in getting amongst the houses and gardens, but with the French advance close on our heels. Here, however, observing the chausste full of hussars, they pulled up. Had they continued their charge we were gone, for these hussars were scattered about the road in the utmost confusion, some in little squads, others singly, and, moreover, so crowded together that we had no room whatever to act with any effect - either they or us.

"Meantime the enemy's detachments began to envelop the gardens, which Lord Uxbridge observing, called to me, 'Here, follow me with two of your guns,' and immediately himself led the way into one of the narrow lanes between the gardens. What he intended doing, God knows, but I obeyed. The lane was very little broader than our carriages - there was not room for a horse to have passed them! The distance from the chaussee to the end of the lane, where it debouched on the open fields, could scarcely have been above one or two hundred yards at most. His lordship and I were in front, the guns and mounted detachments following. What he meant to do I was at a loss to conceive; we could hardly come to action in the lane; to enter on the open was certain destruction. Thus we had arrived at about fifty yards from its termination when a body of chasseurs or hussars appeared there as if waiting for us. These we might have seen from the first, for nothing but a few elder bushes intercepted the view from the chaussee.

"The whole transaction appears to me so wild and confused that at times I can hardly believe it to have been more than a confused dream - yet true it was - the general-in-chief of the cavalry exposing himself amongst the skirmishers of his rearguard, and literally doing the duty of a cornet! 'By God! we are all prisoners' (or some such words), exclaimed Lord Uxbridge, dashing his horse at one of the garden-banks, which he cleared, and away he went, leaving us to get out of the scrape as best we could. There was no time for hesitation - one manoeuvre alone could extricate us if allowed time, and it I ordered. ' Reverse by unlimbering ' was the order. To do this the gun was to be unlimbered, then turned round, and one wheel run up the bank, which just left space for the limber to pass it. The gun is then limbered up again and ready to move to the rear. The execution, however, was not easy, for the very reversing of the limber itself in so narrow a lane, with a team of eight horses, was sufficiently difficult, and required first-rate driving.

"Nothing could exceed the coolness and activity of our men; the thing was done quickly and well, and we returned to the chaussee without let or hindrance. How we were permitted to do so, I am at a loss to imagine; for although I gave the order to reverse, I certainly never expected to have seen it executed. Meantime my own situation was anything but a pleasant one, as I sat with my back to the gentlemen at the end of the lane, whose interference I momentarily expected, casting an eye from time to time over my shoulder to ascertain whether they still kept their position. There they sat motionless, and although thankful for their inactivity, I could not but wonder at their stupidity. It seemed, however, all of a piece that day - all blunder and confusion ; and this last I found pretty considerable on regaining the chaussee. His lordship we found collecting the scattered hussars together into a squadron for our rescue, for which purpose it was he had so unceremoniously left us. Heavy as the rain was and thick the weather, yet the French could not but have seen the confusion we were in, as they had closed up to the entrance of the enclosure; and yet they did not at once take advantage of it.

"Things could not remain long in this state. A heavy column of cavalry approached us by the chaussee, whilst another skirting the enclosures, appeared pushing forward to cut us off. Retreat now became imperative. The order was given, and away we went, helter-skelter - guns, gun-detachments, and hussars all mixed pele-mele, going like mad, and covering each other with mud, to be washed off by the ram, which, before sufficiently heavy, now came down again as it had done at first, in splashes instead of drops, soaking us anew to the skin, and, what was worse, extinguishing every slow match in the brigade. The obscurity caused by the splashing of the rain was such, that at one period I could not distinguish objects more than a few yards distant. Of course we lost sight of our pursuers altogether, and the shouts and halloos,

BLUCHER

and even laughter, they had at first sent forth were either silenced or drowned in the uproar of the elements and the noise of our too rapid retreat ; for in addition to everything else the crashing and rattling of the thunder were most awful, and the glare of the lightning blinding. In this state we gained the bridge of Genappe at the moment when the thunder-cloud, having passed over, left us in comparative fine weather, although still raining heavily.

"For the last mile or so we had neither seen nor heard anything of our lively French friends, and now silently wound our way up the deserted street, nothing disturbing its death-like stillness save the iron sound of horses' feet, the rumbling of the carriages, and the splashing of water as it fell from the eaves - all this was stillness compared with the hurly-burly and din from which we had just emerged.

"On gaining the high ground beyond the town, we suddenly came in sight of the main body of our cavalry drawn up across the chaussee in two lines, and extending away far to the right and left of it. It would have been an imposing spectacle at any time, but just now appeared to me magnificent, and I hailed it with complacency, for here I thought our fox-chase must end. 'Those superb Life Guards and Blues will soon teach our pursuers a little modesty.' Such fellows! - surely nothing can withstand them. Scarcely had these thoughts passed through my mind ere an order from his lordship recalled us to the rear. The enemy's horse artillery, having taken up a position in the meadows near the bridge, were annoying our dragoons as they debouched from the town. The ground was heavy from the rain, and very steep, so that it was only by great exertion that we succeeded at last in getting our guns into the adjoining field.

"The moment we appeared the French battery bestowed on us its undivided attention, which we quickly acknowledged by an uncommonly well-directed fire of spherical case. Whilst so employed, Major M'Donald came up and put me through a regular catechism as to length of fuse, whether out of bag A or B, &c., &c. Although much vexed at such a schooling just now, yet the major appeared so seriously in earnest that I could not but be amused; however, to convince him that we knew what we were about, I directed his attention to our excellent practice, so superior to that of our antagonist, who was sending all his shot far over our heads. The French seemed pretty well convinced of this too, for after standing a few rounds they quitted the field, and left us again without occupation. The major vanishing at the same time, I sent my guns, &c., to the rear, and set off to join Lord Uxbridge, who was still fighting hi the street. Our ammunition was expended the waggons having been taken away by Sir Augustus Frazer at Quatre Bras.

"On regaining my troop I found Major M'Donald and the rockets with it. They were in position on a gentle elevation, on which likewise were formed the lines of cavalry stretching across the chaussde. Immediately on our left, encased in the hollow road, the Blues were formed in close column of half-squadrons, and it was not long ere Lord Uxbridge, with those he had retained at Genappe, came sweeping over the hill and joined us. They were closely followed by the French light cavalry, who, descending into the hollow, commenced a sharp skirmish with our advance-posts. Soon squadron after squadron appeared on the hill we had passed, and took up their positions, forming a long line parallel to ours, whilst a battery of horse artillery, forming across the chaussee, just on the brow of the declivity, opened its fire on us, though without much effect. To this we responded, though very slowly, having no more ammunition than what remained in our limbers.

"In order to amuse the enemy and our own cavalry, as well as to prevent the former noticing the slackness of our fire, I proposed to Major M'Donald making use of the rockets, which had hitherto done nothing. There was a little hesitation about this, and one of the officers (Strangways) whispered me, 'No, no it's too far!' This I immediately told the Major, proposing as a remedy that they should go closer. Still there was demur; but at last my proposition was agreed to, and down they marched into the thick of the skirmishers in the bottom. Of course, having proposed the measure myself, I could do no less than accompany them.

"Whilst they prepared their machinery, I had time to notice what was going on to the right and left of us. Two double lines of skirmishers extended all along the bottom - the foremost of each line were within a few yards of each other - constantly in motion, riding backwards and forwards, firing their carbines or pistols, and then reloading, still on the move. This fire seemed to me more dangerous for those on the hills above than for us below; for all, both French and English, generally stuck out their carbines or pistols as they continued to move backwards and forwards, and discharged them without taking any particular aim, and mostly in the air. I did not see a man fall on either side. The thing appeared quite ridiculous, and but for hearing the bullets whizzing overhead, one might have fancied it no more than a sham-fight.

"Meanwhile the rocketeers had placed a little iron triangle in the road with a rocket lying on it. The order to fire is given, portfire applied; the fidgety missile begins to sputter out sparks and wriggle its tail for a second or so, and then darts forth straight up the chaussee. A gun stands right in its way, between the wheels of which the shell in the head of the rocket bursts; the gunners fall right and left; and those of the other guns, taking to their heels, the battery is deserted in an instant. Strange; but so it was. I saw them run, and for some minutes afterwards I saw the guns standing mute and unmanned, whilst our rocketeers kept shooting off rockets, none of which ever followed the course of the first ; most of them, on arriving about the middle of the ascent, took a vertical direction, whilst some actually turned back upon ourselves ; and one of these, following me like a squib until its shell exploded, actually put me in more danger than all the fire of the enemy throughout the day. Meanwhile the French artillerymen, seeing how the land lay, returned to their guns and opened a fire of case-shot on us, but without effect, for we retreated to our ridge without the loss of a man, or even any wounded, though the range could not have been above 200 yards.

"As we had overtaken the rear of our infantry, it became necessary to make a stand here to enable them to gain ground. Major M'Donald therefore sent me in pursuit of my ammunition waggons, since all in our limbers was expended. Having before sent for these, we calculated that they could not now be very far off. In going to the rear, I passed along the top of the bank, under which, as I have said, the Blues were encased in the hollow road. Shot and shells were flying pretty thickly about just then, and sometimes striking the top of the bank would send down a shower of mud and clods upon them.

"The ammunition waggons I found coming up, and was returning with them when I met my whole troop again retiring by the road, whilst the cavalry did so by alternate regiments across the fields. The ground offering no feature for another stand, we continued thus along the road. The infantry had made so little progress that we again overtook the rear of their column, composed of Brunswickers - some of those same boys I used to see practising at Schapdale in my rides to Brussels. These poor lads were pushing on at a great rate. As soon as their rear divisions heard the sound of our horses' feet, without once looking behind them, they began to crowd and press on those in front, until at last, hearing us close up to them, and finding it impossible to push forward in the road, many of them broke off into the fields; and such was their panic that, in order to run lighter, away went arms and knapsacks in all directions, and a general race ensued, the whole corps being in the most horrid confusion. It was to no purpose that I exerted my little stock of German to make them understand we were their English friends. A frightened glance and away, was all the effect of my interference, which drove many of them off."

The retreat came to an end here. The rearguard, without knowing it, had reached the low ridge running east and west across the Brussels road, where Wellington had resolved to make his final stand, and where the greatest battle in modern history was on the morrow to be fought:-

"We did not long remain idle, for the guns were scarcely loaded ere the rear of our cavalry came crowding upon the infantry corps we had passed, and which were then only crossing the valley, the French advance skirmishing with these, whilst their squadrons occupied the heights. We waited a little until some of their larger masses were assembled, and then opened our fire with a range across the valley of about 1200 yards. The echo of our first gun had not ceased when, to my astonishment, a heavy cannonade, commencing in a most startling manner from behind our hedge, roiled along the rising ground, on part of which we were posted. The truth now flashed on me; we had rejoined the army, and it is impossible to describe the pleasing sense of security I felt at having now the support of something more staunch than cavalry.

"The French now brought up battery after battery, and a tremendous cannonading was kept up by both sides for some time. The effect was grand and exciting. Our position was a happy one, for all their shot which grazed

CHARGE OF THE FRENCH LANCERS AT WATERLOO

short came and struck in the perpendicular bank of our gravel-pit, and only one struck amongst us, breaking the traversing handspike at one of the guns, but injuring neither man nor horse. Our fire was principally directed against their masses as we could see them, which was not always the case from the smoke that, for want of wind, hung over them; then against their smaller parties that had advanced into the valley to skirmish with the rearguard of our cavalry.

"Here, for the second and last time, I saw Napoleon, though infinitely more distant than in the morning. Some of my non-commissioned officers pointed their guns at the numerous cortege accompanying him as they stood near the road by Belle Alliance; and one, pointed by old Quartermaster Hall, fell in the midst of them. At the moment we saw some little confusion amongst the group, but it did not hinder them from continuing the reconnaissance.

"Whilst we were thus engaged, a man of no very prepossessing appearance came rambling amongst our guns, and entered into conversation with me on the occurrences of the day. He was dressed in a shabby old drab greatcoat and a rusty round hat. I took him at the time for some amateur from Brussels (of whom we had heard there were several hovering about), and thinking many of his questions rather impertinent, was somewhat short in answering him, and he soon left us. How great was my astonishment on learning soon after that this was Sir Thomas Picton! The enemy, finding us obstinate in maintaining our position, soon slackened, and then ceased firing altogether ; and we were immediately ordered to do the same, and establish ourselves in bivouac for the night.

"Thoroughly wet - cloaks, blankets, and all - comfort was out of the question, so we prepared to make the best of it. Our first care was, of course, the horses, and these we had ample means of providing for, since, in addition to what corn we had left, one of our men had picked up and brought forward on an ammunition waggon a large sackful, which he found in the road near Genappe. Thus they, at least, had plenty to eat, and having been so well drenched all day, were not much in need of water. For ourselves we had nothing! - absolutely nothing! - and looked forward to rest alone to restore our exhausted strength. Rather a bore going supperless to bed after such a day, yet was there no help for it.

"Our gunners, &c., soon stowed themselves away beneath the carriages, using the painted covers as additional shelter against the rain, which now set in again as heavy as ever. We set up a small tent, into which (after vain attempts at procuring food or lodgings in the farm or its out buildings, all of which were crammed to suffocation with officers and soldiers of all arms and nations) we crept, and rolling ourselves in our wet blankets, huddled close together, in hope, wet as we were, and wet as the ground was, of keeping each other warm. I know not how my bedfellows got on, as we all lay for a long while perfectly still and silent - the old Peninsular hands disdaining to complain before their Johnny Newcome comrades, and these fearing to do so lest they should provoke such remarks, as 'Lord have mercy on your poor tender carcass! what would such as you have done in the Pyrenees?' or 'Oho, my boy! this is but child's play to what we saw in Spain.' So all who did not sleep (I believe the majority) pretended to do so, and bore their suffering with admirable heroism.

"For my part, I once or twice, from sheer fatigue, got into something like a doze; yet it would not do. There was no possibility of sleeping, for, besides being already so wet, the tent proved no shelter, the water pouring through the canvas in streams; so up I got, and to my infinite joy, found that some of the men had managed to make a couple of fires, round which they were sitting smoking their short pipes in something like comfort. The hint was a good one, and at that moment my second captain joining me, we borrowed from them a few sticks, and choosing the best spot under the hedge, proceeded to make a fire for ourselves. In a short time we succeeded in raising a cheerful blaze, which materially bettered our situation. My companion had an umbrella (which, by the way, had afforded some merriment to our people on the march) ; this we planted against the sloping bank of the hedge, and seating ourselves under it, he on one side of the stick, I on the other, we lighted cigars and became - comfortable. Dear weed ! what comfort, what consolation dost thou not impart to the wretched! - with thee a hovel becomes a palace. What a stock of patience is there not enveloped in one of thy brown leaves!

"And thus we sat enjoying ourselves, puffing forth into the damp night air streams of fragrant smoke, being able now deliberately to converse on what had been and probably would be. All this time a most infernal clatter of musketry was going on, which, but for the many quiet dark figures seated round the innumerable fires all along the position, might have been construed into a night attack. But as these gentlemen were between us and the enemy we felt assured of timely warning, and ere long learned that all this proceeded as before from the infantry discharging and cleaning their pieces.

"Whilst so employed, a rustling in the hedge behind attracted our attention, and in a few minutes a poor fellow belonging to some Hanoverian regiment, wet through like everybody else, and shivering with cold, made his appearance, and modestly begged permission to remain a short time and warm himself by our fire. He had somehow or other wandered from his colours, and had passed the greater part of the night searching for them, but in vain. At first he appeared quite exhausted, but the warmth reinvigorating him, he pulled out his pipe and began to smoke. Having finished his modicum and carefully disposed of the ashes, he rose from his wet seat to renew his search, hoping to find his corps before daylight, he said, lest it should be engaged. Many thanks he offered for our hospitality; but what was our surprise when, after fumbling in his haversack for some time, he pulled out a poor half-starved chicken, presented it to us, and marched off. This was a Godsend, in good truth, to people famished as we were; so calling for a camp-kettle, our prize was on the fire in a twinkling.

"Our comrades in the tent did not sleep so soundly but that they heard what was going on, and the kettle was hardly on the lire ere my gentlemen were assembled round it, a wet and shivering group, but all eager to partake of our good fortune - and so eager that after various betrayals of impatience, the miserable chicken was at last snatched from the kettle ere it was half-boiled, pulled to pieces and speedily devoured. I got a leg for my share, but it was not one mouthful, and this was the only food I tasted since the night before."

CHAPTER V
WATERLOO

Mercer's account of Waterloo has much less of literary art and skill in it than other parts of his book. He plunges the reader, without warning and without explanation, into the roar of the great fight. His description of the ground and of the position of the army is thrust, as a sort of parenthesis, into the middle of the story of the actual struggle. Mercer's troop was stationed till long past noon in reserve on the British right. The battle to Mercer was nothing but an incessant and deep-voiced roar of guns, a vision of drifting smoke, in which would appear at times dim figures of charging horsemen, or outlines of infantry squares, edged with steel and flame, and out of which flowed tiny processions of wounded, trickling backwards over the ridge in front. About three o'clock, however, the troop was suddenly brought up to the battle-line, at a point where it was in imminent peril of giving way. From that moment Mercer was in the smoky, tormented, thunder-shaken vortex of the great fight, and his description of it is graphic and impressive in the highest degree. This is how the morning of Waterloo dawned for Mercer and his gunners:-

"June 18 - Memorable day! Some time before daybreak the bombardier who had been despatched to Langeveldt returned with a supply of ammunition.

"With the providence of an old soldier, he had picked up and Drought on

SHAW AT WATERLOO

a considerable quantity of beef, biscuit, and oatmeal, of which there was abundance scattered about everywhere. Casks of rum, &c., there were, and having broached one of these - he and his drivers - every one filled his canteen - a most considerate act, and one for which the whole troop was sincerely thankful. Nor must I omit to remark that, amidst such temptations, his men had behaved with the most perfect regularity, and returned to us quite sober! The rum was divided on the spot; and surely if ardent spirits are ever beneficial, it must be to men situated as ours were; it therefore came most providentially. The oatmeal was converted speedily into stirabout, and afforded our people a hearty meal, after which all hands set to work to prepare the beef, make soup, &c. Unfortunately, we preferred waiting for this, and passed the stirabout, by which piece of folly we were doomed to a very protracted fast, as will be seen.

"Whilst our soup was cooking, it being now broad daylight, I mounted my horse to reconnoitre our situation. During the night another troop (I think Major Ramsay's) had established itself in our orchard, and just outside the hedge I found Major Bean's, which had also arrived during the night, direct from England. Ascending from the farm towards the ground we had left yesterday evening, the face of the slope, as far as I could see, to the right and left, was covered with troops en bivouac - here, I think, principally cavalry. Of these some were cleaning their arms, some cooking, some sitting round fires smoking, and a few, generally officers, walking about or standing hi groups conversing. Many of the latter eagerly inquired where I was going, and appeared very anxious for intelligence, all expecting nothing less than to recommence our retreat. I continued on to the position we had occupied last, and thence clearly saw the French army on the opposite hill, where everything appeared perfectly quiet - people moving about individually, and no formation whatever. Their advanced-posts and vedettes in the valley, just beyond La Haye Sainte, were also quiet.

"Having satisfied my curiosity I returned the way I came, communicating my observations to the many eager inquirers I met with. Various were the speculations in consequence. Some thought the French were afraid to attack us, others that they would do so soon, others that the Duke would not wait for it, others that he would, as he certainly would not allow them to go to Brussels; and so they went on speculating, whilst I returned to my people. Here, finding the mess not yet ready, and nothing to be done, I strolled into the garden of the farm, where several Life Guardsmen were very busy digging potatoes - a fortunate discovery, which I determined to profit by. Therefore, calling up some of my men, to work we went without loss of time."

It is amusing to notice that Mercer was so busy digging potatoes that he quite failed to observe that the battle had actually commenced! His senses were buried in the potato-hillocks! So the regiments fell into line, the batteries moved off to their assigned places, the French guns began to speak,

BATTLE OF MONT SAINT-JEAN OR THE BATTLE OF WATERLOO
Colored litho by Antoine Charles Horace Vernet - called Carle Vernet (1758 - 1836) and Jacques François Swebach (1769-1823)

and Waterloo had begun; and though Mercer stood on the very edge of the field, he took no notice of the rise of the curtain on the great tragedy. He says:-

"Whilst thus employed I noticed a very heavy firing going on in front, but this did not make us quit our work. Shortly after, to my great astonishment, I observed that all the bivouacs on the hillside were deserted, and that even Ramsay's troop had left the orchard without my being aware of it, and my own was left quite alone, not a soul being visible from where I stood in any direction, the ground they had quitted presenting one unbroken muddy solitude. The firing became heavier and heavier. Alarmed at being thus left alone, when it was evident something serious was going on, I hastened back and ordered the horses to be put to immediately.

"Away went our mess untasted. One of the servants was desired to hang the kettle with its contents under an ammunition waggon. The stupid fellow hung the kettle as desired, but first emptied it. Without orders, and all alone, the battle (for now there was no mistaking it) going on at the other side of the hill, I remained for a few minutes undecided what to do. It appeared to me we had been forgotten. All, except only ourselves, were evidently engaged, and labouring under this delusion, I thought we had better get into the affair at once. As soon, therefore, as the troop was ready I led them up the hill on the high-road, hoping to meet some one who could give me directions what to do."

The tragedy of the battle soon made itself visible, in very dramatic shape, to Mercer:-

"We had not proceeded a hundred yards, when an artillery officer came furiously galloping down towards us. It was Major M'Lloyd, in a dreadful state of agitation - such, indeed, that he could hardly answer my questions. I learned, however, that the battle was very serious and bloody. Their first attack had been on that part of our position where his battery stood ; but now the principal efforts were making against our right. All this was told in so hurried and anxious a manner, that one could hardly understand him. 'But where are you going?' he added. I told him my plan. 'Have you no orders?' 'None whatever; I have not seen a soul.' 'Then, for God's sake, come and assist me, or I shall be ruined. My brigade is cut to pieces, ammunition expended, and, unless reinforced, we shall be destroyed.'

He was dreadfully agitated, and when I took his hand and promised to be with him directly, seemed trans- ported with joy; so, bidding me make haste, he darted up the hill again, and went to receive that death-stroke which, ere long, was to terminate his earthly career. I trust before that termination he heard the reason why I never fulfilled that promise; for weeks elapsed ere he died, no doubt - otherwise he must have set me down for a base poltroon. My destiny led me elsewhere. My tutelary spirit was at hand: the eternal Major M'Donald made his appearance, and, giving me a sharp reprimand for having quitted my bivouac, desired me instantly to return to the foot of the hill, and there wait for orders.

"Sulkily and slowly we descended, and forming in line on the ground opposite the farm of Mont St. Jean, with our left to the road, I dismounted the men that they might be a little less liable to be hit by shot and shells which, coming over the hill, were continually plunging into the muddy soil all around us. This was a peculiarly dismal situation - without honour or glory, to be knocked on the head in such a solitude, for not a living being was in sight.

" It was while thus standing idle that a fine, tall, upright old gentleman, in plain clothes, followed by two young ones, came across our front at a gallop from the Brussels road, and continued on towards where we sup- posed the right of our army to be. I certainly stared at seeing three unarmed civilians pressing forward into so hot a fight. These were the Duke of Richmond and his two sons. How long we had been in this position, I know not, when at length we were relieved from it by our adjutant (Lieutenant Bell), who brought orders for our removal to the right of the second line. Moving, therefore, to our right, along the hollow, we soon began a very gentle ascent, and at the same time became aware of several corps of infantry, which had not been very far from us, but remained invisible, as they were all lying down. Although in this move we may be said to have been always under a heavy fire, from the number of missiles flying over us, yet were we still so fortunate as to arrive in our new position without losing man or horse."

Now Mercer at last got a glimpse of the whole landscape of the great fight. But even when looking at Waterloo, and to an accompaniment of flying lead, Mercer has an eye for the picturesque, not to say the Pastoral:-

"In point of seeing, our situation was much improved; but for danger and inactivity, it was much worse, since we were now fired directly at, and positively ordered not to return the compliment - thc object in bringing us here being to watch a most formidable-looking line of lancers drawn up opposite to us, and threatening the right flank of our army.

"To the right we looked over a fine open country, covered with crops and interspersed with thickets or small woods. There all was peaceful and smiling, not a living soul being in sight. To our left, the main ridge terminated rather abruptly just over Hougoumont, the back of it towards us being broken ground, with a few old trees on it just where the Nivelle road descended between high banks into the ravine. Thus we were formed en potence with the first line, from which we (my battery) were separated by some hundred yards. In our rear the 14th Regiment of infantry (in square, I think) lay on the ground. In our front were some light dragoons of the German Legion, who from time to time detached small parties across the ravine. These pushed cautiously up the slope towards the line of lancers to reconnoitre.

THE GRENADIER OF THE OLD GUARD
Jean Baptiste Edouard Detaille (1847–1912)

"The corn, down to the edge of the ravine nearer the Nivelle road and beyond it, was full of French riflemen; and these were warmly attacked by others from our side of the ravine, whom we saw crossing and gradually working their way up through the high corn, the French as gradually retiring. On the right of the lancers, two or three batteries kept up a continued fire at our position ; but their shot, which could have been only 4-pounders, fell short - many not even reaching across the ravine. Some, however, did reach their destination ; and we were particularly plagued by their howitzer shells with long fuses, which were continually falling about us, and lay spitting and spluttering several seconds before they exploded, to the no small annoyance of man and horse. Still, however, nobody was hurt ; but a round-shot, striking the ammunition boxes on the body of one of our waggons, penetrated through both and lodged in the back of the rear one, with nearly half its surface to be seen from without - a singular circumstance! In addition to this front fire, we were exposed to another on our left flank - the shot that passed over the main ridge terminating their career with us.

"Having little to occupy us here, we had ample leisure to observe what was passing there. We could see some corps at the end near us in squares - dark masses, having guns between them, relieved from a background of grey smoke, which seemed to fill the valley beyond, and rose high in the air above the hill. Every now and then torrents of French cavalry of all arms came sweeping over the ridge, as if carrying all before them. But, after their passage, the squares were still to be seen in the same places ; and these gentry, who we feared would next fall on us, would evaporate, nobody could well say how. The firing still increased in intensity, so that we were at a loss to conjecture what all this could mean.

"About this time, being impatient of standing idle, and annoyed by the batteries on the Nivelle road, I ventured to commit a folly, for which I should have paid dearly, had our Duke chanced to be in our part of the field. I ventured to disobey orders, and open a slow deliberate fire at the battery, thinking with my 9-pounders soon to silence his 4-pounders. My astonishment was great, however, when our very first gun was responded to by at least half-a-dozen gentlemen of very superior calibre, whose presence I had not even suspected, and whose superiority we immediately recognised by their rushing noise and long reach, for they flew far beyond us. I instantly saw my folly, and ceased firing, and they did the same - the 4-pounders alone continuing the cannonade as before. But this was not all. The first man of my troop touched was by one of these confounded long shots. I shall never forget the scream the poor lad gave when struck. It was one of the last they fired, and shattered his left arm to pieces as he stood between the waggons. That scream went to my very soul, for I accused myself as having caused his misfortune. I was, however, obliged to conceal my emotion from the men, who had turned to look at him; so, bidding them 'stand to their front,' I

THE SUNKEN ROAD AT WATERLOO
Stanley Berkley, from 'A History of the Nineteenth Century, Year by Year' by Edwin Emerson, Jr., 1902.

continued my walk up and down, whilst Hitchins ran to his assistance.

"Amidst such stirring scenes, emotions of this kind are but of short duration ; what occurred immediately afterwards completely banished Gunner Hunt from my recollection. As a counterbalance to this tragical event, our firing produced one so comic as to excite all our risibility. Two or three officers had lounged up to our guns to see the effect. One of them was a medico, and he (a shower having just come on) carried an umbrella overhead. No sooner did the heavy answers begin to arrive amongst us, than these gentlemen, fancying they should be safer with their own corps, although only a few yards in the rear, scampered off in double-quick, doctor and all, he still carrying his umbrella aloft. Scarcely, however, had he made two paces, when a shot, as he thought, passing rather too close, down he dropped on his hands and knees - or, I should rather say, hand and knees, for the one was employed in holding the silken cover most pertinaciously over him - and away he scrambled like a great baboon, his head turned fearfully over his shoulder, as if watching the coming shot, whilst our fellows made the field resound with their shouts and laughter."

At this point Mercer indulges in some reflections which illustrate, in a striking fashion, the confusion of a great battle, and the difficulty with which even those who are actors in it can describe what took place. It is not merely that a battle-field, by its area, and the fashion in which the all-obscuring smoke drifts over it, evades clear vision and description. The actors in the fight are themselves in such a mood of excitement, and are so passionately preoccupied by their own part in the combat and the scenes immediately about them, that no brain remains sufficiently cool and detached to take in the battle-field as a whole:-

"I think I have already mentioned that it was not until some days afterwards that I was able to resume my regular journal, consequently that everything relative to these three days is written from memory. In trying to recollect scenes of this nature, some little confusion is inevitable ; and here I confess myself somewhat puzzled to account for certain facts of which I am positive. For instance, I remember perfectly Captain Bolton's brigade of 9-pounders being stationed to the left of us, somewhat in advance, and facing as we did, consequently not far from the Nivelle road. Bolton came and conversed with me some time, and was called hastily away by his battery commencing a heavy fire. Query - Who, and what was he firing at? That he was himself under a heavy fire there is equally no doubt, for whilst we were not losing a man, we saw many, both of his men and horses, fall, and but a few minutes after leaving me, he was killed himself - this is a puzzle. I have no recollection of any troops attempting to cross the ravine, and yet his fire was in that direction, and I think must have been toward the Nivelle road.

"A distressing circumstance connected with this (shall I confess it?) made even more impression on my spirits than the misfortune of Gunner Hunt. Bolton's people had not been long engaged when we saw the men of the gun next to us unharness one of the horses and chase it away, wounded, I supposed; yet the beast stood and moved with firmness, going from one carriage to the other, whence I noticed he was always eagerly driven away.

At last two or three gunners drove him before them to a considerable distance, and then returned to their guns. I took little notice of this at the time and was surprised by an exclamation of horror from some of my people in the rear. A sickening sensation came over me, mixed with a deep feeling of pity, when within a few paces of me stood the poor horse in question, side by side with the leaders of one of our ammunition waggons, against which he pressed his panting sides, as though eager to identify himself as of their society - the driver, with horror depicted on every feature, endeavouring by words and gestures (for the kind-hearted lad could not strike) to drive from him so hideous a spectacle.

"A cannon-shot had completely carried away the lower part of the animal's head, immediately below the eyes, till he lived, and seemed fully conscious of all around, whilst his full, clear eye seemed to implore us not to chase him from his companions. I ordered the farrier (Price) to put him out of misery, which, in a few minutes he reported having accomplished, by running his sabre into the animal's heart. Even he evinced feeling on this occasion.

"Meantime the roar of cannon and musketry in the main position never slackened ; it was intense, as was the smoke arising from it. Amidst this, from time to time, was to be seen still more dense columns of smoke rising straight into the air like a great pillar, then spreading out a mushroom head. These arose from the explosions of ammunition waggons, which were continually taking place, although the noise which filled the whole atmosphere was too overpowering to allow them to be heard."

By this time the great French cavalry charges were in full course. Some 10,000 of the finest cavalry in the world were being flung on the stubborn British squares, which, as the French horsemen swept round them, seemed swallowed up in a tossing sea of helmets and gleaming swords and heads of galloping horses. The spray, so to speak, of that fierce human sea, was flung on the spot where Mercer and his gunners stood:-

"Amongst the multitudes of French cavalry continually pouring over the

LE DERNIER GRENADIER DE WATERLOO (THE LAST GRENADIER OF WATERLOO)
Horace Vernet 1789–1863

front ridge, one corps came sweeping down the slope entire, and was directing its course straight for us, when suddenly a regiment of light dragoons (I believe of the German Legion) came up from the ravine at a brisk trot on their flank. The French had barely time to wheel up to the left and push their horses into a gallop when the two bodies came into collision. They were at a very short distance from us, so that we saw the charge perfectly. There was no check, no hesitation on either side; both parties seemed to dash on in a most reckless manner, and we fully expected to have seen a horrid crash - no such thing! Each, as if by mutual consent, opened their files on coming near, and passed rapidly through each other, cutting and pointing, much in the same manner one might pass the fingers of the right hand through those of the left. We saw but few fall. The two corps reformed afterwards, and in a twinkling both disappeared, I know not how or where.

"It might have been about two o'clock when Colonel Gould, R.A., came to me - perhaps a little later. Be that as it may, we were conversing on the subject of our situation, which appeared to him rather desperate. He remarked that in the event of a retreat there was but one road, which no doubt would be instantly choked up, and asked my opinion. My answer was, 'It does indeed look very bad; but I trust in the Duke, who, I am sure, will get us out of it somehow or other.' Meantime gloomy reflections arose in my mind, for though I did not choose to betray myself (as we spoke before the men), yet I could not help thinking that our affairs were rather desperate, and that some unfortunate catastrophe was at hand. In this case I made up my mind to spike my guns and retreat over the fields, draught-horses and all, in the best manner I could, steering well from the high-road and general line of retreat.

"We were still talking on this subject when suddenly a dark mass of cavalry appeared for an instant on the main ridge, and then came sweeping down the slope in swarms, reminding me of an enormous surf bursting over the prostrate hull of a stranded vessel, and then running, hissing and foaming up the beach. The hollow space became in a twinkling covered with horsemen, crossing, turning, and riding about in all directions, apparently without any object. Sometimes they came pretty near us, then would retire a little. There were lancers amongst them, hussars, and dragoons - it was a complete melee. On the main ridge no squares were to be seen; the only objects were a few guns standing in a confused manner, with muzzles in the air, and not one artilleryman. After caracoling about for a few minutes, the crowd began to separate and draw together in small bodies, which continually increased; and now we really apprehended being overwhelmed, as the first line had apparently been. For a moment an awful silence pervaded that part of the position to which we anxiously turned our eyes. 'I fear all is over,' said Colonel Gould, who still remained with me. The thing seemed but too likely, and this time I could not withhold my assent to his remark, for it did indeed appear so.

"Meantime the 14th, springing from the earth, had formed their square, whilst we, throwing back the guns of our right and left divisions, stood waiting in momentary expectation of being enveloped and at- tacked. Still they lingered in the hollow, when suddenly loud and repeated shouts (not English hurrahs) drew our attention to the other side. There we saw two dense columns of infantry pushing forward at a quick pace towards us, crossing the fields, as if they had come from Merke Braine. Every one both of the 14th and ourselves pronounced them French, yet still we delayed opening fire on them. Shouting, yelling, singing, on they came right for us; and being now not above 800 or 1000 yards distant, it seemed folly allowing them to come nearer unmolested. The commanding officer of the 14th to end our doubts rode forwards and endeavoured to ascertain who they were, but soon returned assuring us they were French. The order was already given to fire, when luckily Colonel Gould recognised them as Belgians. Meantime, whilst my attention was occupied by these people, the cavalry had all vanished, nobody could say how or where.

"We breathed again. Such was the agitated state in which we were kept in our second position. A third act was about to commence of a much more stirring and active nature."

Now came, and in a dramatic fashion, the summons which brought troop G into the very front of the fight; and from this point Mercer's story is clear, sustained, and vivid:-

"It might have been, as nearly as I can recollect, about 3 P.M. when Sir Augustus Frazer galloped up, crying out, 'Left limber up, and as fast as you can.' The words were scarcely uttered when my gallant troop stood as desired in column of sub-divisions, left in front, pointing towards the main ridge. 'At a gallop, march! 'and away we flew, as steadily and compactly as if at a review.

LES GRENADIERS À CHEVAL - THE FRENCH CAVALRY AT WATERLOO

"I rode with Frazer, whose face was as black as a chimney-sweep's from the smoke, and the jacket-sleeve of his right arm torn open by a musket-ball or case- shot, which had merely grazed his flesh. As we went along he told me that the enemy had assembled an enormous mass of heavy cavalry in front of the point to which he was leading us (about one-third of the distance between Hougoumont and the Charleroi road), and that in all probability we should immediately be charged on gaining our position. 'The Duke's orders, however, are positive,' he added, 'that in the event of their persevering and charging home, you do not expose your men, but retire with them into the adjacent squares of infantry.' As he spoke we were ascending the reverse slope of the main position. We breathed a new atmosphere - the air was suffocatingly hot, resembling that issuing from an oven. We were enveloped in thick smoke, and, malgré the incessant roar of cannon and musketry, could distinctly hear around us a mysterious humming noise, like that which one hears of a summer's evening proceeding from myriads of black beetles;

cannon-shot, too, ploughed the ground in all directions, and so thick was the nail of balls and bullets that it seemed dangerous to extend the arm lest it should be torn off.

"In spite of the serious situation in which we were, I could not help being somewhat amused at the astonishment expressed by our kind-hearted surgeon (Hitchins), who heard for the first time this sort of music. He was close to me as we ascended the slope, and hearing this infernal carillon about his ears, began staring round in the wildest and most comic manner imaginable, twisting himself from side to side, exclaiming, 'My God, Mercer, what is that? What is all this noise? How curious!-how very curious!' And then when a cannon-shot rushed hissing past, 'There!-there! What is it all!' It was with great difficulty that I persuaded him to retire; for a time he insisted on remaining near me, and it was only by pointing out how important it was to us, in case of being wounded, that" he should keep himself safe to be able to assist us, that I prevailed on him to withdraw. Amidst this storm we gained the summit of the ridge, strange to say, without a casualty; and Sir Augustus, pointing out our position between two squares of Brunswick infantry, left us with injunctions to remember the Duke's order, and to economise our ammunition.

"The Brunswickers were falling fast - the shot every moment making great gaps in their squares, which the officers and sergeants were actively employed in filling up by pushing their men together, and sometimes thumping them ere they could make them move. These were the very boys whom I had but yesterday seen throwing away their arms, and fleeing, panic-stricken, from the very sound of our horses' feet Today they fled not bodily, to be sure, but spiritually, for their senses seemed to have left them. There they stood, with recovered arms, like so many logs, or rather like the very wooden figures which I had seen them practising at in their cantonments. Every moment I feared they would again throw down their arms and flee; but their officers and sergeants behaved nobly, not only keeping them together, but managing to keep their squares close in spite of the carnage made amongst them. To have sought refuge amongst men in such a state were madness - the very moment our men ran from their guns, I was convinced, would be the signal for their disbanding. We had better, then, fall at our posts than in such a situation.

" Our coming up seemed to re-animate them, and all their eyes were directed to us - indeed, it was providential, for, had we not arrived as we did, I scarcely think there is a doubt of what would have been their fate. That the Duke was ignorant of their danger I have from Captain Baynes, our brigade-major, who told me that after Sir Augustus Frazer had been sent for us, his Grace exhibited considerable anxiety for our coming up; and that when he saw us crossing the fields at a gallop, and in so compact a body, he actually cried out, 'Ah! that's the way I like to see horse artillery move.'"

Then follows perhaps the most spirited description of a duel betwixt guns and horsemen - from the gunner's point of view - to be found in English literature:-

"Our first gun had scarcely gamed the interval between their squares, when I saw through the smoke the leading squadrons of the advancing column coming on at a brisk trot, and already not more than one hundred yards distant, if so much, for I don't think we could have seen so far. I immediately ordered the line to be formed for action - case-shot! and the leading gun was unlimbered and commenced firing almost as soon as the word was given; for activity and intelligence our men were unrivalled.

"The very first round, I saw, brought down several men and horses. They continued, however, to advance. I glanced at the Brunswickers, and that glance told me it would not do; they had opened a fire from their front faces, but both squares appeared too unsteady, and I resolved to say nothing about the Duke's order, and take our chance - a resolve that was strengthened by the effect of the remaining guns as they rapidly succeeded in coming to action, making terrible slaughter, and in an instant covering the ground with men and horses. Still they persevered in approaching us (the first round had brought them to a walk), though slowly, and it did seem they would ride over

THE BATTLE OF WATERLOO
William Heath

us. We were a little below the level of the ground on which they moved, having in front of us a bank of about a foot and a half or two feet high, along the top of which ran a narrow road - and this gave more effect to our case-shot, all of which almost must have taken effect, for the carnage was frightful. The following extract, from a related account of a conscript, translated from the French and published by Murray, is so true and exact as to need no comment: 'Through the smoke I saw the English gunners abandon their pieces, all but six guns stationed under the road, and almost immediately our cuirassiers were upon the squares, whose fire was drawn in zigzags. Now, I thought, those gunners would be cut to pieces; but no, the devils kept firing with grape, which mowed them down like grass.'

"I suppose this state of things occupied but a few seconds, when I observed symptoms of hesitation, and in a twinkling, at the instant I thought it was all over with us, they turned to either flank and filed away rapidly to the rear. Retreat of the mass, however, was not so easy. Many facing about and trying to force their way through the body of the column, that part next to us became a complete mob, into which we kept a steady fire of case-shot from our six pieces. The effect is hardly conceivable, and to paint this scene of slaughter and confusion impossible. Every discharge was followed by the fall of numbers, whilst the survivors struggled with each other, and I actually saw them using the pommels of their swords to fight their way out of the melee. Some, rendered desperate at finding themselves thus pent up at the muzzles of our guns, as it were, and others carried away by their horses, maddened with wounds, dashed through our intervals - few thinking of using their swords, but pushing furiously onward, intent only on saving themselves. At last the rear of the column, wheeling about, opened a passage, and the whole swept away at a much more rapid pace than they had advanced, nor stopped until the swell of the ground covered them from our fire. We then ceased firing; but as they were still not far off, for we saw the tops of their caps, having reloaded, we stood ready to receive them should they renew the attack.

"One of, if not the first man who fell on our side was wounded by his own gun. Gunner Butterworth was one of the greatest pickles in the troop, but at the same time a most daring, active soldier; he was No.7 (the man who sponged, &c.) at his gun. He had just finished ramming down the shot, and was stepping back outside the wheel when his foot stuck in the miry soil, pulling him forward at the moment the gun was fired. As a man naturally does when falling, he threw out both his arms before him, and they were blown off at the elbows. He raised himself a little on his two stumps, and looked up most piteously in my face. To assist him was impossible - the safety of all, everything, depended upon not slackening our fire, and I was obliged to turn from him. The state of anxious activity in which we were kept all day, and the numbers who fell almost immediately afterwards, caused me to lose sight of poor Butterworth; and I afterwards learned that he had succeeded in rising, and was gone to the rear; but on inquiring for him next day, some of my people who had been sent to Waterloo told me that they saw his body lying by the roadside near the farm of Mont St. Jean - bled to death.

WELLINGTON AT WATERLOO Robert Alexander Hillingford

The retreat of the cavalry was succeeded by a shower of shot and shells, which must have annihilated us had not the little bank covered and threw most of them over us. Still some reached us and knocked down men and horses.

"At the first charge the French column was composed of grenadiers à cheval* and cuirassiers, the former in front. I forget whether they had or had not changed this disposition, but think, from the number of cuirasses we found afterwards, that the cuirassiers led the second attack. Be this as it may, their column re- assembled. They prepared for a sccond attempt, sending up a cloud of skirmishers, who galled us terribly by a fire of carbines and pistols at scarcely forty yards from our front."

Betwixt the cavalry rushes came little intervals of waiting, while the

** These grenadiers à cheval were very fine troops, clothed in blue uniforms without facings, cuffs, or collars. Broad - very broad - buff belts, and huge muff caps, made them appear gigantic fellows.*

broken squadrons re-formed in the valley below, and the breathless gunners on the ridge renewed their ammunition. These pauses gave the French skirmishers - who had crept close up to the guns - their chance, and which were more trying to the British gunners than even the wild onfall of the horsemen:-

"We were obliged to stand with port-fires lighted, so that it was not without a little difficulty that I succeeded in restraining the people from firing, for they grew impatient under such fatal results. Seeing some exertion beyond words necessary for this purpose, I leaped my horse up the little bank, and began a promenade (by no means agreeable) up and down our front, without even drawing my sword, though these fellows were within speaking distance of me. This quieted my men; but the tall blue gentlemen, seeing me thus dare them, immediately made a target of me, and commenced a very deliberate practice, to show us what very bad shots they were, and verify the old artillery proverb, 'The nearer the target, the safer you are.' One fellow certainly made me flinch, but it was a miss; so I shook my finger at him and called him coquin, &c. The rogue grinned as he reloaded, and again took aim. I certainly felt rather foolish at that moment, but was ashamed after such bravado to let him see it, and therefore continued my promenade. As if to prolong my torment, he was a terrible time about it. To me it seemed an age. Whenever I turned, the muzzle of his infernal carbine still followed me. At length bang it went, and whiz came the ball close to the back of my neck, and at the same instant down dropped the leading driver of one of my guns (Miller), into whose forehead the cursed missile had penetrated.

"The column now once more mounted the plateau, and these popping gentry wheeled off right and left to clear the ground for their charge. The spectacle was imposing, and if ever the word sublime was appropriately applied, it might surely be to it. On they came in compact squadrons, one behind the other, so numerous that those of the rear were still below the brow when the head of the column was but at some sixty or seventy yards from our guns. Their pace was a slow but steady trot. None of your furious galloping charges was this, but a deliberate advance at a deliberate pace, as of men resolved to carry their point. They moved in profound silence, and the only sound that could be heard from them amidst the incessant roar of battle was the low, thunder-like reverberation of the ground beneath the simultaneous tread of so many horses.

"On our part was equal deliberation. Every man stood steadily at his post, the guns ready, loaded with a round-shot first and a case over it; the tubes were in the vents; the port-fires glared and spluttered behind the wheels; and my word alone was wanting to hurl destruction on that goodly show of gallant men and noble horses. I delayed this, for experience had given me confidence. The Brunswickers partook of this feeling, and with their squares - much reduced in point of size - well closed, stood firmly with arms at the recover, and eyes fixed on us, ready to commence their fire with our first discharge. It was indeed a grand and imposing spectacle. The column was led on this time by an officer in a rich uniform, his breast covered with decorations, whose earnest gesticulations were strangely contrasted with the solemn demeanour of those to whom they were addressed. I thus allowed them to advance unmolested until the head of the column might have been about fifty or sixty yards from us, and then gave the word 'Fire!' The effect was terrible, nearly the whole leading rank fell at once ; and the round-shot, penetrating the column, carried confusion throughout its extent. The ground, already encumbered with victims of the first struggle, became now almost impassable. Still, however, these devoted warriors struggled on, intent only on reaching us. The thing was impossible.

"Our guns were served with astonishing activity, whilst the running fire of the two squares was maintained with spirit. Those who pushed forward over the heap of carcasses of men and horses gained but a few paces in advance, there to fall in their turn and add to the difficulties of those succeeding them. The discharge of every gun was followed by a fall of men and horses like that of grass before the mower's scythe. When the horse alone was killed, we could see the cuirassiers divesting themselves of the encumbrance and

NAPOLEON BAONAPARTE, 1812
Jacques-Louis David (1748–1825)

making their escape on foot. Still, for a moment the confused mass (for all order was at an end) stood before us, vainly trying to urge their horses over the obstacles presented by their fallen comrades, in obedience to the now loud and rapid vociferations of him who had led them on and remained unhurt.

"As before, many cleared everything and rode through us ; many came plunging forward only to fall, man and horse, close to the muzzles of our guns; but the majority again turned at the very moment when, from having less ground to go over, it was safer to advance than retire, and sought a passage to the rear. Of course the same confusion, struggle amongst themselves, and slaughter prevailed as before, until gradually they disappeared over the brow of the hill. We ceased firing, glad to take breath. Their retreat exposed us, as before, to a shower of shot and shells: these last, falling amongst us, with very long fuses, kept burning and hissing a long time before they burst, and were a considerable annoyance to man and horse. The bank in front, however, again stood our friend, and sent many over us innocuous."

Here is a picture of what may be called the human atmosphere of the battle in its later stages, the high- strung nerves, the weariness, the exhaustion of passion, the carelessness of close-pressing death, the fast-following alternation of deadly peril and of miraculous escape:-

"Lieutenant Breton, who had already lost two horses, and had mounted a troop-horse, was conversing with me during this our leisure moment. As his horse stood at right angles to mine, the poor jaded animal dozingly rested his muzzle on my thigh; whilst I, the better to hear amidst the infernal din, leant forward, resting my arm between his ears. In this attitude a cannon-shot smashed the horse's head to atoms. The headless trunk sank to the ground - Breton looking pale as death, expecting, as he afterwards told me, that I was cut in two. What was passing to the right and left of us I know no more about than the man in the moon not even what corps were beyond the Brunswickers. The smoke confined our vision to a very small compass, so

LIFE GUARDS CHARGING AT THE BATTLE OF WATERLOO
Richard Caton Woodville (1856–1927)

that my battle was restricted to the two squares and my own battery; and, as long as we maintained our ground, I thought it a matter of course that others did so too.

"It was just after this accident that our worthy commanding officer of artillery, Sir George Adam Wood, made his appearance through the smoke a little way from our left flank. As I said, we were doing nothing, for the cavalry were under the brow re-forming for a third attack, and we were being pelted by their artillery. 'D-n it, Mercer,' said the old man, blinking as a man does when facing a gale of wind, 'you have hot work of it here.' 'Yes, sir, pretty hot;' and I was proceeding with an account of the two charges we had already discomfited, and the prospect of a third, when, glancing that way, I perceived their leading squadron already on the plateau. 'There they are again,' I exclaimed; and, darting from Sir George sans cérémonie, was just in time to meet them with the same destruction as before. This time, indeed, it was child's play. They could not even approach us in any decent order, and we fired most deliberately; it was folly having attempted the thing.

"I was sitting on my horse near the right of my battery as they turned and began to retire once more. Intoxicated with success, I was singing out, 'Beautiful!-beautiful!' and my right arm was nourishing about, when some one from behind, seizing it, said quietly, 'Take care, or you'll strike the Duke;' and in effect our noble chief, with a serious air, and apparently much fatigued, passed close by me to the front, without seeming to take the slightest notice of the remnant of the French cavalry still lingering on the ground. This obliged us to cease firing; and at the same moment I - perceiving a line of infantry ascending from the rear, slowly, with ported arms, and uttering a sort of feeble, suppressed hurrah, ankle-deep in a thick, tenacious mud, and threading their way amongst or stepping over the numerous corpses covering the ground, out of breath from their exertions, and hardly preserving a line, broken everywhere into large gaps the breadth of several files - could not but meditate on the probable results of the last charge had I, in obedience to the Duke's order, retired my men into the squares and allowed the daring and formidable squadrons a passage to our rear, where they must have gone thundering down on this disjointed line. The summit gained, the line was amended, files closed in, and the whole, including our Brunswickers, advanced down the slope towards the plain.

"Although the infantry lost several men as they passed us, yet on the whole the cannonade began to slacken on both sides (why, I know not), and, the smoke clearing away a little, I had now, for the first time, a good view of the field. On the ridge opposite to us dark masses of troops were stationary, or moving down into the intervening plain. Our own advancing infantry were hid from view by the ground. We therefore recommenced firing at the enemy's masses, and the cannonade, spreading, soon became general again along the line."

Mercer, so far, had been fighting sabres with 12-pounders, and all the advantage had been on his side. He had inflicted enormous damage on the enemy, and suffered little himself. But now the enemy's guns began to speak, and Mercer's battery was smitten by a cruel and continuous flank fire, which practically destroyed it:-

"Whilst thus occupied with our front, we suddenly became sensible of a most destructive flanking fire from a battery which had come, the Lord knows how, and established itself on a knoll somewhat higher than the ground we stood on, and only about 400 or 500 yards a little in advance of our left flank. The rapidity and precision of this fire were quite 'appalling. Every shot almost took effect, and I certainly expected we should all be annihilated. Our horses and limbers being a little retired down the slope, had hitherto been somewhat under cover from the direct fire in front; but this plunged right amongst them, knocking them down by pairs, and creating horrible confusion. The drivers could hardly extricate themselves from one dead horse ere another fell, or perhaps themselves. The saddle-bags, in many instances, were torn from the horses' backs, and their contents scattered over the field. One shell I saw explode under the two finest wheel-horses in the troop - down they dropped. In some instances the horses of a gun or ammunition waggon remained, and all their drivers were killed.*

"The whole livelong day had cost us nothing like this. Our gunners, too - the few left fit for duty of them - were so exhausted that they were unable to run the guns up after firing, consequently at every round they retreated nearer to the limbers; and as we had pointed our two left guns towards the people who were annoying us so terribly, they soon came altogether in a confused heap, the trails crossing each other, and the whole dangerously near the limbers and ammunition waggons, some of which were totally unhorsed, and others in sad confusion from the loss of their drivers and horses, many of them lying dead in their harness attached to their carriages. I sighed for my poor troop - it was already but a wreck.

"I had dismounted, and was assisting at one of the guns to encourage my poor exhausted men, when through the smoke a black speck caught my eye, and I instantly knew what it was. The conviction that one never sees a shot coming towards you unless directly in its line flashed across my mind, together with the certainty that my doom was sealed. I had barely time to exclaim 'Here it is, then!' - much in that gasping sort of way one does when going into very cold water, takes away the breath 'whush' it went past my face, striking the point of my pelisse collar, which was lying open, and smash

* *"The field was so much covered with blood, that it appeared as if it had been flooded with it," &c. - Simpsons 'Paris after Waterloo,' &c., p.21*

into a horse close behind me. I breathed freely again.

"Under such a fire, one may be said to have had a thousand narrow escapes; and, in good truth, I frequently experienced that displacement of air against my face, caused by the passing of shot close to me; but the two above recorded, and a third, which I shall mention, were remarkable ones, and made me feel in full force the goodness of Him who protected me among so many dangers. Whilst in position on the right of the second line, I had reproved some of my men for lying down when shells fell near them until they burst. Now my turn came. A shell, with a long fuse, came slop into the mud at my feet, and there lay fizzing and flaring to my infinite discomfiture. After what I had said on the subject, I felt that I must act up to my own words, and, accordingly, there I stood, endeavouring to look quite composed until the cursed thing burst - and, strange to say, without injuring me, though so near. The effect on my men was good."

But was it really a French battery which was wrecking Mercer's guns? Or, in the mad inevitable distraction of a great battle were the Allied gunners destroying each other? Mercer's story leaves this point in a state of very disquieting doubt:-

"We had scarcely fired many rounds at the enfilading battery, when a tall man in the black Brunswick uniform came galloping up to me from the rear, exclaiming, 'Ah! Mine Gott! Mine Gott! Vat is it you doos, sare? Dat is your friends de Proosiens; an you kills dem! Ah! Mine Gott! Mine Gott; vil you no stop, sare? Vil you no stop? Ah! Mine Gott, mine Gott! Vat for is dis? De Inglish kills dere friends de Proosiens! Vere is de Dook von Vellington? Vere is de Dock von Vellington? Ah! Mine Gott! Minc Gott!' &c., &c., and so he went on raving like one demented. I observed that if these were our friends the Prussians, they were treating us very uncivilly; and that it was not without sufficient provocation we had turned our guns on them, pointing out to him at the same time the bloody proofs of my assertion.

"Apparently not noticing what I said, he continued his lamentations, and, 'Vil you no stop, sare, I say? 'Wherefore, thinking he might be right, to pacify him I ordered the whole to cease firing, desiring him to remark the consequences. Psieu, psieu, psieu, came our 'friends' 'shots, one after another; and our friend himself had a narrow escape from one of them. 'Now, sir,' I said, 'you will be convinced ; and we will continue our firing, whilst you can ride round the way you came, and tell them they kill their friends the English; the moment their fire ceases, so shall mine.' Still he lingered, exclaiming, 'Oh, dis is terreeble to see de Proosien and de Inglish kill von anoder!'

"At last, darting off, I saw no more of him. The fire continued on both sides, mine becoming slacker and slacker, for we were reduced to the last extremity, and must have been annihilated but for the opportune arrival of a battery of Belgic artillery a little on our left, which, taking the others in flank nearly at point blank, soon silenced and drove them oft". We were so reduced that all our strength was barely sufficient to load and fire three guns out of our six.

"These Belgians were all beastly drunk, and, when they first came up, not at all particular as to which way they fired; and it was only by keeping an eye on them that they were prevented treating us, and even one another. The wretches had probably already done mischief elsewhere - who knows?"

CHAPTER VI
AFTER THE FIGHT

Mercer could hardly tell when and how Waterloo began, and he can almost as little tell when and how it ended! So wild is the confusion, so overwhelming the excitement of a great battle for the actors in it:-

"My recollections of the later part of this day are rather confused; I was fatigued and almost deaf. I recollect clearly, however, that we had ceased firing, the plain below being covered with masses of troops, which we could not distinguish from each other. Captain Walcot of the Horse Artillery, had come to us, and we were all looking out anxiously at the movements below and on the opposite ridge, when he suddenly shouted out, 'Victory!-victory! they fly!-they fly!' and sure enough we saw some of the masses dissolving, as it were, and those composing, them streaming away in confused crowds over the field, whilst the already desultory fire of their artillery ceased altogether.

"I shall never forget this joyful moment! - this moment of exultation! On looking round, I found we were left almost alone. Cavalry and infantry had all moved forward, and only a few guns here and there were to be seen on the position. A little to our right were the remains of Major M'Donald's troop under Lieutenant Sandilands, which had suffered much, but nothing like us. We were congratulating ourselves on the happy results of the day when an aide-de-camp rode up, crying, 'Forward, sir! forward! It is of the utmost importance that this movement should be supported by artillery!' at the same time waving his hat much in the manner of a huntsman laying on his dogs. I smiled at his energy, and, pointing to the remains of my poor troop, quietly asked, 'How, sir?' A glance was sufficient to show him the impossibility, and away he went.

"Our situation was indeed terrible. Of 200 fine horses with which we had entered the battle, upwards of 140 lay dead, dying, or severely wounded. Of the men, scarcely two-thirds of those necessary for four guns remained, and these so completely exhausted as to be totally incapable of further exertion. Lieutenant Breton had three horses killed under him; Lieutenant Hincks was wounded in the breast by a spent ball; Lieutenant Leathes on the hip by a splinter; and although untouched myself, my horse had no less than eight wounds, one of which, a graze on the fetlock joint, lamed him for ever. Our guns and carriages were, as before mentioned, altogether in a confused heap, intermingled with dead and wounded horses, which it had not been possible to disengage from them.

"My poor men, such at least as were untouched, fairly worn out, their clothes, faces, &c., blackened by the smoke and spattered over with mud and blood, had seated themselves on the trails of the carriages, or had thrown themselves on the wet and polluted soil, too fatigued to think of anything but gaining a little rest. Such was our situation when called upon to advance. It was impossible, and we remained where we were. For myself, I was also excessively tired, hoarse to making speech painful, and deaf from the infernal uproar of the last eleven hours. Moreover, I was devoured by a burning thirst, not a drop of liquid having passed my lips since the evening of the 16th; but although, with the exception of the chicken's leg last night, I may be said to have eaten nothing for two whole days, yet did I not feel the least desire for food."

When the battle was over, Mercer's artistic sensibilities - his eye for landscape, his sense of sky-effects and of natural beauty - awoke. He was perhaps the only man in Wellington's army who could study cloud-effects in the night-sky, which looked down on the slain of Waterloo, or contemplate, with botanical discrimination and approval, the plants in the garden at Hougoumont the next morning:-

The evening had become fine, and but for an occasional groan or lament

THE WATERLOO BANQUET, 1836
William Salter

from some poor sufferer, and the repeated piteous neighing of wounded horses, tranquility might be said to reign over the field. As it got dusk, a large body of Prussian artillery arrived, and formed their bivouac near us. There was not light to see more of them than that their brass guns were kept bright, and that their carriages were encumbered with baggage, and, besides, appeared but clumsy machines when compared with ours. All wore their greatcoats, which apparently they had marched in. As they looked at us rather scowlingly, and did not seem inclined to hold any communication with us, I soon returned to my own people, whom I found preparing to go supperless to bed - the two remaining officers, the non-commissioned officers, and men having all got together in a heap, with some painted covers spread under, and others drawn over them - at a distance from our guns, &c., the neighbourhood of which they said, was too horrible to think of sleeping there.

"For my part, after standing all day amongst all these horrors, I felt no squeamishness about sleeping amongst them; so pulling down the painted cover of a limber over the footboard in the manner of a tent roof, I crept under

THE DEFENCE OF HOUGOUMONT

it and endeavoured to sleep. The cramped situation in which I lay, and the feverish excitement of my mind, forbade, however, my obtaining that sound and refreshing sleep so much needed; I only dozed.

From one of these dozes I awoke about midnight, chilled and cramped to death from the awkward doubled-up position imposed upon me by my short and narrow bed. So up I got to look around and contemplate a battlefield by the pale moonlight.

"The night was serene and pretty clear; a few light clouds occasionally passing across the moon's disc, and throwing objects into transient obscurity, added considerably to the solemnity of the scene. Oh, it was a thrilling sensation thus to stand in the silent hour of the night and contemplate that field - all day long the theatre of noise and strife, now so calm and still - the actors prostrate on the bloody soil, their pale wan faces upturned to the moon's cold beams, which caps and breastplates, and a thousand other things, reflected back in brilliant pencils of light from as many different points! Here and there some poor wretch, sitting up amidst the countless dead, busied himself in endeavours to stanch the flowing stream with which his life was fast ebbing away. Many whom I saw so employed that night were, when morning dawned, lying stiff and tranquil as those who had departed earlier. From time to time a figure would half raise itself from the ground, and then, with a despairing groan, fall back again. Others, slowly and painfully rising, stronger, or having less deadly hurt, would stagger away with uncertain steps across the field in search of succour.

"Many of these I followed with my gaze until lost hi the obscurity of distance; but many, alas! after staggering a few paces, would sink again on the ground with their entrails hanging out and yet I gazed! Horses, too, there were to claim our pity - mild, patient, enduring. Some lay on the ground with their entrails hanging out, and yet they lived. These would occasionally attempt to rise, but like their human bedfellows, quickly falling back again, would lift their poor heads, and, turning a wistful gaze at their side, lie quietly down again, to repeat the same until strength no longer remained, and then, their eyes gently closing, one short convulsive struggle closed their sufferings. One poor animal excited painful interest - he had lost, I believe, both his hind-legs ; and there he sat the long night through on his tail, looking about, as if in expectation of coming aid, sending forth, from time to time, long and protracted melancholy neighing. Although I knew that killing him at once would be mercy, I could not muster courage even to give the order. Blood enough I had seen shed during the last six-and-thirty hours, and sickened at the thought of shedding more. There, then, he still sat when we left the ground, neighing after us, as if reproaching our desertion of him in the hour of need."

After the storm of a great battle has rolled away it leaves behind a wreckage - human and animal - of a very amazing sort; and of the wreckage of Waterloo Mercer gives a grimly vivid description. The effect is that of one of Vereschagin's pictures translated into literary terms:-

"June 19 - The cool air of the morning lasted not long; the rising sun soon burst in all his glory over our bloody bivouac, and all nature arose into renewed life, except the victims of ambition which lay unconscious of his presence. I had not been up many minutes when one of my sergeants came to ask if they might bury Driver Crammond. 'And why particularly Driver Crammond?' 'Because he looks frightful, sir; many of us have not had a wink of sleep for him.' Curious! I walked to the spot where he lay, and certainly a more hideous sight cannot be imagined. A cannon-shot had carried away the whole head except barely the visage, which still remained attached to the torn and bloody neck. The men said they had been prevented sleeping by seeing his eyes fixed on them all night; and thus this one dreadful object had superseded all the other horrors by which they were surrounded. He was of course immediately buried, and as immediately forgotten.

"Our first care after this was to muster the remaining force, to disentangle our carriages from each other, and from the dead and dying animals with which they were encumbered. Many sound or only slightly wounded horses, belonging to different corps of both armies, were wandering about the field. Of these we caught several in the course of the morning, and thus collected, with what remained of our own fit for work, sufficient to horse four guns, three ammunition waggons, and the forge. Of men we had nearly enough for these at reduced numbers, so we set to work equipping ourselves without delay. Although supplies of ammunition had been sent to us during the action, yet little remained. The expenditure had been enormous. A return had been called for yesterday evening just as we were lying down to rest, but, fatigued as we all were it was impossible to give this correctly. As near as I could ascertain, we must have fired nearly 700 rounds per gun. Our harness, &c., was so cut to pieces, that but for the vast magazines around us from which we could pick and choose we should never have got off the field.

"Soon after daybreak an officer came from head-quarters to desire me to send all my superfluous carriages to Lillois, where a park was forming, and to inform me that a supply of ammunition would be found in the village of

THE BATTLE OF WATERLOO

NAPOLEON'S LAST GRAND ATTACK AT WATERLOO
Ernest Crofts

Waterloo. Accordingly the carriages were sent without delay; but this requiring all the horses, they were obliged to make a second trip for the ammunition. Whilst this was doing I had leisure to examine the ground in our immediate vicinity. Books and papers, &c., covered it in all directions. The books at first surprised me, but upon examination the thing was explained. Each French soldier, it appeared, carried a little accompt-book of his pay, clothing, &c., &c. The scene was now far from solitary ; for numerous groups of peasants were moving about busily employed stripping the dead, and perhaps finishing those not quite so. Some of these men I ,met fairly staggered under the enormous load of clothes, &c., they had collected. Some had firearms, swords, &c., and many had large bunches of crosses and decorations ; all seemed in high glee, and professed unbounded hatred of the French.

"I had fancied we were almost alone on the field, seeing only the remains of Major Bull's troop of horse artillery not far from us (the Prussians had gone forward about or a little before daybreak); but in wandering towards the Charleroi road I stumbled on a whole regiment of British infantry fast asleep, in columns of divisions, wrapped in their blankets, with their knapsacks for pillows. Not a man was awake. There they lay in regular ranks, with the officers and sergeants in their places, just as they would stand when awake. Not far from these, in a little hollow beneath a white thorn, lay two Irish light-infantry men sending forth such howlings and wailings and oaths and execrations as were shocking to hear. One of them had his leg shot off, the other a thigh smashed by a cannon-shot. They were certainly pitiable objects, but their vehement exclamations, &c., were so strongly contrasted with the quiet, resolute bearing of hundreds both French and English around them, that it blunted one's feelings considerably.

"I tried in vain to pacify them; so walked away amidst a volley of abuse as a hard-hearted wretch who could thus leave two poor fellows to die like dogs.

"What could I do? All, however, though in more modest terms, craved assistance; and every poor wretch begged most earnestly for water. Some of my men had discovered a good well of uncontaminated water at Hougoumont and filled their canteens, so I made several of them accompany me and administer to the most craving in our immediate vicinity. Nothing could exceed their gratitude, or the fervent blessings they implored on us for this momentary relief. The French were in general particularly grateful; and those who were strong enough entered into conversation with us on the events of yesterday, and the probable fate awaiting themselves. All the non-commissioned officers and privates agreed in asserting that they had been deceived by their officers and betrayed; and, to my surprise, almost all of them reviled Bonaparte as the cause of their misery.

"Many begged me to kill them at once, since they would a thousand times rather die by the hand of a soldier than be left at the mercy of those villainous Belgic peasants. Whilst we stood by them several would appear consoled and become tranquil; but the moment we attempted to leave, they invariably renewed the cry, 'Ah, Monsieur, tuez moi donc! Tuez moi, pour 1'amour de Dieu!' &c., &c. It was in vain I assured them carts would be sent to pick them all up. Nothing could reconcile them to the idea of being left. They looked on us as brother soldiers, and knew we were too honourable to harm them: 'But the moment you go, those vile peasants will first insult and then cruelly murder us.' This, alas! I knew, was but too true.

"One Frenchman I found in a far different humour - an officer of lancers, and desperately wounded; a strong, square-built man, with reddish hair and speckled complexion. When I approached him he appeared suffering horribly - rolling on his back, uttering loud groans. My first impulse was to raise and place him in a sitting posture; but, the moment he was touched, opening his eyes and seeing me, he became perfectly furious. Supposing he mistook my intention, I addressed him in a soothing tone, begging he would allow me to render him what little assistance was in my power. This only seemed to irritate him the more; and on my presenting him the canteen with water, he dashed it from him with such a passionate gesture and emphatic 'Non!' that I saw there was no use in teasing, and therefore reluctantly left him.

"Returning towards our position, I was forcibly struck by the immense heap of bodies of men and horses which distinguished it even at a distance; indeed, Sir Augustus Frazer told me the other day, at Nivelles, that in riding over the field, 'he could plainly distinguish the position of G troop from the opposite height by the dark mass which, even from that distance, formed a remarkable feature in the field.' These were his very words. One interesting sufferer I had nearly forgotten. He was a fine young man of the grenadiers à cheval, who had lain groaning near us all night - indeed, scarcely five paces from my bed; therefore was the first person I visited as soon as daylight came. He was a most interesting person - tall, handsome, and a perfect gentleman in manners and speech; yet his costume was that of a private soldier. We conversed with him some time, and were exceedingly pleased with his mild and amiable address. Amongst other things he told us that

WILLIAM II OF ORANGE

Marshal Ney had led the charges against us.

"I now began to feel somewhat the effects of my long fast in a most unpleasant sense of weakness and an inordinate craving for food, which there was no means of satisfying. My joy, then, may be imagined when, returning to our bivouac, I found our people returned from Lillois, and, better still, that they had brought with them a quarter of veal, which they had found in a muddy ditch, of course in appearance then filthy enough. What was this to a parcel of men who had scarcely eaten a morsel for three days? In a trice it was cut up, the mud having been scraped off with a sabre, a fire kindled and fed with lance-shafts and musket-stocks; and old Quartermaster Hall, under- taking the cooking, proceeded to fry the dirty lumps in the lid of a camp-kettle. How we enjoyed the savoury smell! and, having made ourselves seats of cuirasses* piled upon each other, we soon had that most agreeable of animal gratifications - the filling our empty stomachs. Never was a meal more perfectly military, nor more perfectly enjoyed."

By this time the artillery officer in Mercer was exhausted, the botanist and artist began to emerge, and he strolls off to visit, as a sort of country gentleman at leisure, the garden at Hougoumont! He says:-

"Having despatched our meal and then the ammunition waggons to Waterloo, and leaving the people employed equipping as best they could, I

* *"Here were more cuirasses than men, for the wounded (who could move), divesting themselves of its encumbrance, had made their escape, leaving their armour on the ground where they had fallen."*

BATTLE OF WATERLOO - 18 JUNE 1815
Jan Willem Pieneman

set off to visit the chateau likewise; for the struggle that had taken place there yesterday rendered it an object of interest. The same scene of carnage as elsewhere characterised that part of the field over which I now bent my steps. The immediate neighbourhood of Hougoumont was more thickly strewn with corpses than most other parts of the field - the very ditches were full of them. The trees all about were most woefully cut and splintered both by cannon shot and musketry. The courts of the chateau presented a spectacle more terrible even than any I had yet seen. A large barn had been set on fire, and the conflagration had spread to the offices and even to the main building. Here numbers, both of French and English, had perished in the flames, and their blackened swollen remains lay scattered about in all directions. Amongst this heap of ruins and misery many poor devils yet remained alive, and were sitting up endeavouring to bandage their wounds. Such a scene of horror, and one so sickening, was surely never witnessed.

"Two or three German dragoons were wandering among the ruins, and many peasants. One of the former was speaking to me when two of the latter, after rifling the pockets, &c., of a dead Frenchman, seized the body by the shoulders, and raising it from the ground, dashed it down again with all their force, uttering the grossest abuse, and kicking it about the head and face - revolting spectacle! - doing this, no doubt, to court favour with us. It had a contrary effect, which they soon learned. I had scarcely uttered an exclamation of disgust, when the dragoon's sabre was flashing over the miscreants' heads, and hi a moment descended on their backs and shoulders with such vigour that they roared again, and were but too happy to make their escape. I turned from such scenes and entered the garden. How shall I describe the delicious sensation I experienced!

"The garden was an ordinary one, but pretty - long straight walks of turf overshadowed by fruit-trees, and between these beds of vegetables, the whole enclosed by a tolerably high brick wall. Is it necessary to define my sensations? Is it possible that I am not understood at once? Listen, then. For the last three days I have been in a constant state of excitement - in a perfect fever. My eyes have beheld nought but war in all its horrors - my ears have been assailed by a continued roar of cannon and cracking of musketry, the shouts of multitudes and the lamentations of war's victims. Suddenly and unexpectedly I find myself in solitude, pacing a green avenue, my eyes refreshed by the cool verdure of trees and shrubs; my ears soothed by the melody of feathered songsters - yea, of sweet Philomel Herself - and the pleasing hum of insects sporting in the genial sunshine. Is there nothing in this to excite emotion? Nature in repose is always lovely: here, and under such circumstances, she was delicious. Long I rambled in this garden, up one walk, down another, and thought I could dwell here contented for ever.

"Nothing recalled the presence of war except the loop holed wall and two or three dead Guardsmen*; but the first caused no interruption, and these last lay so concealed amongst the exuberant vegetation of turnips and cabbages,

* *In some accounts of the battle and vista to the field, &c., it has been stated that this garden was a scene of slaughter. Totally untrue! As I have stated in the text, I did not see above two or three altogether. There certainly might have been more concealed amongst the vegetation, but they could not have been many.*

&c., that, after coming from the field of death without, their pale and silent forms but little deteriorated my enjoyment. The leaves were green, roses and other flowers bloomed forth in all their sweetness, and the very turf when crushed by my feet smelt fresh and pleasant. There was but little of disorder visible to tell of what had been enacted here. I imagine it must have been assailed by infantry alone; and the havoc amongst the trees without made by our artillery posted on the hill above to cover the approach to it principally, perhaps, by Bull's howitzer battery.

"I had satisfied my curiosity at Hougoumont, and was retracing my steps up the hill when my attention was called to a group of wounded Frenchmen by the calm, dignified, and soldier-like oration addressed by one of them to the rest. I cannot, like Livy, compose a fine harangue for my hero, and, of course, I could not retain the precise words, but the import of them was to exhort them to bear their sufferings with fortitude; not to repine, like women or children, at what every soldier should have made up his mind to suffer as the fortune of war, but above all, to remember that they were surrounded by Englishmen, before whom they ought to be doubly careful not to disgrace themselves by displaying such an unsoldier-like want of fortitude.

"The speaker was sitting on the ground, with his lance stuck upright beside him - an old veteran, with a thick, bushy, grizzly beard, countenance like a lion - a lancer of the Old Guard, and no doubt had fought in many a field. One hand was flourished in the air as he spoke, the other, severed at the wrist, lay on the earth beside him; one ball (case-shot, probably) had entered his body, another had broken his leg. His suffering, after a night of exposure so mangled, must have been great; yet he betrayed it not. His bearing was that of a Roman, or perhaps of an Indian warrior, and I could fancy him concluding appropriately his speech in the words of the Mexican king, 'And I too; am I on a bed of roses?'

"In passing Bull's bivouac it was my fate to witness another very interesting scene. A wounded hussar had somehow or other found his way there from another part of the field, and exhausted by the exertion, had just

NAPOLEON AFTER THE BATTLE OF WATERLOO
François Flameng

fainted. Some of those collected round him cried out for water, and a young driver, who, being outside the throng, had not yet seen the sufferer, seized a canteen and ran away to fill it. Whilst he was absent the hussar so far recovered as to be able to sit up. The driver returned at this moment, and pushing aside his comrades, knelt down to enable the hussar to drink, holding the canteen to his lips, and in so doing recognised a brother whom he not seen for years. His emotion was extreme, as may be supposed."

From the narrative of the March to Paris which followed Waterloo, we take only one incident. Mercer is at Nivelles, watching the crowds and the excitement in the streets:-

"Suddenly a loud shout announces something extraordinary even on this day of excitement. Everyone hurries to the spot, pushing each other, jumping, shouting. 'What can it mean?' I inquired. 'Monsieur l'Officier, c'est un convoi des prisonniers que vient d'arrier,' replied my man, doffing at the

THE BATTLEFIELD AT WATERLOO

same time his bonnet de nuit and making a most respectful salaam. I stopped to see the convoy pass. The prisoners, dressed in grey capotes and bonnets de fourrage, marched steadily on. Some vieux moustaches look very grave, and cast about furious glances at the noisy crowd which follows them with the perseverance of a swarm of mosquitoes, sacréing and venting all kind of illiberal abuse on them and the b- of an Emperor. Many, however, younger men, laugh, joke, and return their abuse with interest, whilst the soldiers of the escort (English) March doggedly along, pushing aside the more forward of the throng, and apparently as if only marching round a relief.

"At noon arrived in the neighbourhood of Mons, where we overtook the Greys, Inniskillings, Ross's troop of horse artillery, and several other corps, both of cavalry and infantry. We had, in short, now rejoined the army. The

Greys and the Inniskillings were mere wrecks - the former, I think, did not muster 200 men, and the latter, with no greater strength, presented a sad spectacle of disorganisation and bad discipline; they had lost more than half their appointments. Some had helmets, some had non; many had the skull-cap, but with the crest cut or broken off; many were without, not only belts, but also canteens and haversacks. The enemy surely had not effected in a single day so complete a disorganisation, and I shrewdly suspect these rollicking Paddies of having mainly spoilt themselves. The other corps all looked remarkably well, although they, too, had partaken in the fight.

"We crossed after the Greys, and came with them on the main road to Maubeuge at the moment a Highland regiment (perhaps the 92nd), which had come through Mons, was passing. The moment the Highlanders saw the Greys an electrifying cheer burst spontaneously from the column, which was answered heartily; and on reaching the road the two columns became blended for a few minutes - the Highlanders running to shake hands with their brave associates in the late battle. This burst of feeling was delightful - everybody felt it; and although two or three general officers were present, none interfered to prevent or to censure this breach of discipline."

THE DUKE OF WELLINGTON
ON THE THIRTY-SECOND ANNIVERSARY OF THE BATTLE OF WATERLOO
Pictorial Times, June 19th 1847

MORE FROM THE SAME SERIES

Most books from the 'Military History from Original Sources' series are edited and endorsed by Emmy Award winning film maker and military historian Bob Carruthers, producer of Discovery Channel's Line of Fire and Weapons of War and BBC's Both Sides of the Line. Long experience and strong editorial control gives the military history enthusiast the ability to buy with confidence. The series advisor is David McWhinnie, producer of the acclaimed Battlefield series for Discovery Channel. David and Bob have co-produced books and films with a wide variety of the UK's leading historians including Professor John Erickson and Dr David Chandler.

Where possible the books draw on rare primary sources to give the military enthusiast new insights into a fascinating subject.

The English Civil Wars

The Zulu Wars

Into Battle with Napoleon 1812

Waterloo 1815

The Anglo-Saxon Chronicle

Medieval Warfare

Renaissance Warfare

1914-1918

Sea Battles in the Age of Sail

Sun Tzu - The Art of War

Recollections of the Great War in the Air

Soldier of the Empire

For more information visit www.pen-and-sword.co.uk